974.3

ARCHAEOLOGY IN VERMONT

D1565091

Model showing maple syrup and sugar making by the Ojibways, whose language and customs are Algonkian. Most New England Indians were of Algonkian stock, the chief exception being Iroquoian Mohawks of Northwestern Vermont. Note the hemispherical wigwams.

Courtesy Museum of the American Indian, New York City.

ARCHAEOLOGY IN VERMONT

Some Reviews
Supplemented by Materials from
New England and New York

compiled by JOHN C. HUDEN

REVISED EDITION

The publisher wishes to acknowledge the kindness of
Grace B. Huden and the University of Vermont in
permitting them to reprint this book.

CHARLES E. TUTTLE COMPANY
RUTLAND, VERMONT

Representatives
Continental Europe: BOXERBOOKS, INC., *Zurich*
British Isles: PRENTICE-HALL INTERNATIONAL, INC., *London*
Australasia: PAUL FLESCH & CO., PTY. LTD., *Melbourne*
Canada: M. G. HURTIG LTD., *Edmonton*

Published by the Charles E. Tuttle Company, Inc.
of Rutland, Vermont & Tokyo, Japan
with editorial offices at
Suido 1-chome, 2-6, Bunkyo-ku, Tokyo, Japan

Copyright in Japan, 1971 by Charles E. Tuttle Co., Inc.

Library of Congress Catalog Card No. 74-130409

International Standard Book No. 0-8048-0929-1

First Tuttle edition published 1971

PRINTED IN JAPAN

TABLE OF CONTENTS

Table of Contents (continued)

Table of Contents (continued)

Acknowledgements:

In addition to credits scattered through this work the compiler wishes to thank Mrs. Bonnie Anderson for the drawings of the Bellows Falls rock inscriptions as well as for her aid in preparing and proofreading the manuscripts.

                              /s/   John C. Huden
                                    Compiler

Vermont Archaeology, 1970

Introduction to the New Edition
by William A. Haviland,
Associate Professor of Anthropology, University of Vermont

From the standpoint of archaeology, Vermont has been virtually terra incognita. In the neighboring New England states on the one hand, and New York State on the other, archaeological programs have amassed considerable data on Pre-Columbian culture history. In Vermont, by contrast, archaeological efforts have been sporadic, superficial, and inadequately published. This is unfortunate, for Vermont occupies a key position in the Northeast. On the eve of European penetration, it was a meeting ground between Algonquian and Iroquoian peoples. Before that, it is reasonable to presume that it was a region through which innovations made to the south and west were spread to other peoples of the northeast.

The publication of Huden's book marked the turning point in this situation. It made available an annotated list of the previous publications which dealt with the prehistory of Vermont, immensly simplifying the task of those interested in the subject. Although the methods and/or interpretations represented by most of these sources (C. F. Moorehead, Olson, Perkins) are no longer acceptable in the light of modern archaeological techniques and knowledge, the raw data are still important and useful. Huden's book remains the starting point for anyone who wishes to acquaint himself with the raw material of Vermont archaeology, or who wishes to study the history of archaeological activity in the state.

Since the original publication of Huden's book, a few more publications on Vermont archaeology have appeared (Daniels, 1963; Haviland, 1968; 1969a, 1969b; Hucksoll, 1968; Ritchie, 1965, esp. pp. 85-87 and 131-134). Moreover, the Department of Sociology and Anthropology at the University of Vermont has inaugurated an archaeological survey, in cooperation with the newly formed Vermont Archaeological Society (Morrissey, 1969). This continuing program has developed a system of classification for Vermont's archaeological sites, and aims to compile an inventory of all such sites in the state. Table 1 is a list of those sites (and page references) in Huden's compilation with official site numbers.

TABLE I

Archaeological Sites in the Text

Official Site Number	Name	Page Reference
VT-AD-1	John Donovan Site	7-23
VT-AD-2	Jesse Rivers Site	4-6; 24-32
VT-AD-4	Chipman's Point	3-4; 78-79
VT-AD-5	Fort Cassin	60
VT-AD-12	East Creek	2; 91 ff.; 95 ff.; 97 ff
VT-CH-11	Munson Flats	59-60
VT-FR-1	Swanton Cemetery	44-46; 60; 61; 72; 73
VT-FR-2	Brooks Farm Quarry	72-73; 80-82
VT-FR-3	Reagan Rite	100; 99 ff.
VT-GI-1	Fort Ste. Anne	87
VT-OR-1	Cow Meadow Brook	38; 43
VT-WID-7	Indian Rock, Brattleboro	39; 40
VT-WID-8	Bellows Falls Pictographs	39
VT-WIN-1	North Hartland Site	104

The Vermont Archaeological Society is just starting, as of this writing, to do some site excavation. It publishes an occasional newsletter, and as an affiliate of the Eastern States Archaeological Federation, distributes the bulletin of that organization.

From what has already been done in Vermont, coupled with what is known of the prehistory of surrounding areas, we can begin to see a "bare bones" outline of the state's prehistory. A summary of this may serve to put Huden's sites in perspective. It seems there were two important areas of Pre-Columbian habitation: The Connecticut River Valley and the Champlain Valley. At present, the files of archaeological survey contain records of over 100 sites in these two regions, and new ones will undoubtedly be found. Our knowledge, sketchy though it is, is best for the Champlain Valley, where a considerable chronological spread is represented. In Franklin County is the small campsite of Big Game Hunters who camped on the shores of the Champlain Sea some 9,000 years ago (Table 1: VT-FR-3). The Big Game Hunters seem to have shifted north with the cold zone as warmer postglacial conditions caused ecological changes in the northeast. They were replaced, after a hiatus, by peoples of the Laurentian Archaic culture tradition. These probably filtered into the area just before 2000 B.C. By contrast with the earlier Big Game Hunters, they were hunters of small game, gatherers of wild plant foods, and fishermen. Their remains are especially prominent in the Otter Creek region (Table 1: VT-AD-1 and VT-AD-2, mixed with later material).

The other sites mentioned in Huden are representative of the more recent Woodland tradition, of which Iroquoian and Algonquian cultures were protohistoric representatives. Woodland Culture is an outgrowth of the older Archaic, associated with the introduction of native agriculture, the bow and arrow for hunting, and pottery. Given Vermont's geographical location, it is doubtful that agriculture was ever prominent here. So, in many cases, the Woodland elements may represent a rather thin overlay to a way of life very much like that of the Laurentian Archaic, especially in the case of the Algonquians and their immediate ancestors. While Woodland traits were probably not introduced by migrant peoples arriving in the area, there is evidence for a slightly later influx of outsiders by the third century A.D., who mixed with those already here. The Swanton Cemetery (Table 1: VT-FR-1) is a burial ground of these Adena peoples who apparently did migrate from the Ohio River Valley, and the East Creek site (Table 1: VT-AD-12) is another probable Adena site.

Such is the state of Vermont archaeology ten years after Huden's compilation. In those years, good progress has been made, but there is a long way to go. More careful, scientific excavation is needed. The results of such work need to be widely disseminated. There are presently few exhibits of Vermont artifacts available. Hopefully, to those now housed at the State Historical Society, the Daniels Museum in Orwell, and the Essex Junction office of the Howard National Bank, new and more complete exhibits can be opened to the public. Hopefully, too, by 1980 much more will be known of Vermont's prehistoric past.

REFERENCES

Daniels, Thomas E.
    1963: "Vermont Indians." Journal Press, Poultney, Vermont (available through the State Historical Society, Montpelier).

Haviland, William A.
    1968: The Vermont Site Survey; "Vermont Archaeological
    Society Newsletter," June 1968, Burlington.
    1969a: Excavations at Pine Island. VAS Newsletter,
    No. 2. Vermont Archaeological Society, Burlington.
    1969b: Vermont Hunters, 7000 B.C. Vermont Life, vol.
    24, no. 2, pp. 53-55. Burlington.

Hucksoll, Aurelia C.
    1968: Watercourses and Indian Population in the
    Northeast Kingdom.
    In "Primitive Versus Modern: Contrasting Attitudes
    Toward Environment," George R. Clay, editor, Occasional
    Paper No. 2, Vermont Academy of Arts and Sciences,
    Bennington.

Morrissey, Charles T.
    1969: The Start of V.A.S. "Vermont Life," vol. 24,
    no. 2, p. 52. Burlington.

Ritchie, William A.
    1965: "The Archaeology of New York State." Natural His-
    tory Press, Garden City.

INTRODUCTORY

This bulletin is designed for non-technical people; students, librarians and others who wish to know what archaeological investigations have been attempted in Vermont.

- Scope -

Only the chief endeavors of the past one hundred years have been selected. It is known that amateurish excavations have been attempted from time to time in several Vermont locations, but only "diggings" which have been scientifically conducted have been included; even so, it is probable that some important projects have been overlooked.

- Review Format -

Reviews of several Vermont publications are presented, together with extended mention of some important articles from Maine, New Hampshire, Rhode Island, Connecticut, Massachusetts and New York. Lack of space prevented inclusion of material originating outside of the New York - New England area.

- Illustrations -

Wherever possible, illustrations are used. In one case (the Ground Slate article) suitable pictures are not available; on the other hand, six or seven good photographs of finds at East Creek, Orwell, Addison County, Vt. are set forth although no article describes this major endeavor.

Since the compilation of Archaeology in Vermont, the Vermont Archaeological Society has been formed. Dr. H. Nicholas Muller is secretary of the Society, and the mailing address is Waterman Building, University of Vermont, Burlington, Vermont.

Until some twenty years ago, there was a Champlain Valley Archaeological Society with headquarters at Ticonderoga, N.Y.; the bulk of William A. Ross' fine collection is still at Ft. Ticonderoga. (Not confirmed)

- Indian collection -

Probably the best Indian collection open to the public in Vermont is that of Dr. David Marvin, on display at the Howard National Bank, Essex Junction, Vermont.

The Vermont Historical Society, with headquarters in Montpelier, Vermont, has custody of the Vermont State Collection, which is described in text and plates in Report of the

Vermont State Geologist, 1909-1910, by G. H. Perkins, pp. 1-75. This collection is not on display.

Mr. Thomas E. Daniels, who died in 1962, started a museum next to his home in Orwell, Vermont. "Daniels' Museum" is operated now by Mrs. Daniels. Mr. Daniels book, "Vermont Indians," was published posthumously in 1963 by the Journal Press, Poultney, Vermont.

This information to come from Mrs. Margit Holzinger, Curator of the Fleming Museum, University of Vermont.

- Need for Further Digging -

Archaeologists at The Museum of the American Indian, Heye Foundation, New York City; at the Rochester Museum, Rochester, New York; at the State Museum, Albany, New York and other interested people are unanimous in their statements that new excavations in Vermont would probably yield a rich harvest. Among the places mentioned as probably "good diggings" are Greylock's camp at Swanton; the dunes near Colchester Point; Monkton Pond; Briston Pond; the banks of Lewis and Otter Creeks; West Arlington; the Lake Bomoseen area; West Haven; Lake St. Catherine, Wells, Pownal; Wilmington; Vernon; Brattleboro; Weathersfield Bow; Hartland; Ompompanoosuc; Bradford; Newbury; Peacham; Barnet; Waterford; the Nulhegan river, Bloomfield; the Clyde River, Newport; Derby Line; Canaan and the nearby foothills. In a subsequent bulletin this compiler may augment this list.

At present it is difficult to get owners of possible sites to consent to open their land to archaeologists; and there is no Archaeological Society (nor yet a committee) possessing funds to employ legal counsel, or for purchasing rights-to-dig, much less material and labor for digging. It is to be hoped that there will soon be a resurgence of interest and activity along these lines.

Addison County (Vermont) Artifacts

In the late 1930's the Museum of The American Indian (Heye Foundation, New York City) sponsored extensive diggings at East Creek, Orwell, Addison County, Vermont. Unfortunately the field notes for these works are not available, and apparently no article has ever been written to describe the project. Several photographs exist.

However, through the courtesy of Mr. E. K. Burnett, Director-Emeritus The Museum of the American Indian some fourteen photographs were made available for this compilation; some six are reproduced here.

ARCHAEOLOGY IN VERMONT IN 1938

By John H. Bailey
Archaeologist for Champlain Valley
Archaeological Society
in Residence at the University of Vermont, 1938-39

(Copied from February 1939 Issue of "The Vermont Alumnus")

During 1938, several important steps were taken by the Champlain Valley Archeological Society in unraveling the aboriginal history of that region. Since both of these oc- curred in Vermont, we feel that we are that much closer to a fuller understanding of the primitive peoples who first made their homes in this state.

Below a slightly overhanging cliff of limestone, tower- ing fifty feet above the lake shore, on Chipman's Point, in the township of Orwell, Addison County, we discovered where a crude shelter had extended for almost one hundred feet along the face of the bluff. Excavation proved that at two dif- ferent times groups of Indian people had lived here.

At a time in the distant past, when the talus slope, made by chips and blocks of limestone falling from the cliff in the course of weathering, had reached upward to a spot six feet below where we found it, these early humans first made this their abode and pushed down some of the fallen rock to make a level floor. Onto this floor went the ashes of their camp fires, the bones of the animals they ate, several un- finished notched arrowpoints and chips knocked off in their manufacture. Here against the back wall, these people buried the body of their pet dog, covering him with limestone slabs and camp debris. While here, one of the men of the family must have broken his beautiful highly polished bone dagger. We found five fragments of this implement, tri- angular in section, scattered at this level. It was made from the leg bone of a large animal, perhaps a moose. A short distance away along the back wall, had occurred the burial of a young child. Evidently a favorite child, the parents had placed at the feet a pile of objects consisting of large clam shells, six chisel-like implements in various stages of manufacture out of moose leg bones and a scraper of chert. (A word of explanation regarding the term chert, which material is as near the true flint of Europe as may be obtained locally and equally good as regards its chipping qualities.) Just beyond, they had laid the body of a lynx.

These people then moved away, either up or down the lake, leaving the shelter to the falling rocks and rattlesnakes whose skeletons we found under every large rock. Through the ensuing years, the lime-saturated water dripping from the overhang in certain spots cemented together into large blocks the Indian refuse and limestone chips so that it was physically impossible to remove these and examine the floor level underneath. Perhaps several hundred years later, another group of people, carrying arrows tipped with triangular points and making a good grade of clay pottery jars, noticed the natural advantages of this spot for a home and moved in. The previous inhabitants had used notched arrowpoints and made no pottery so far as we could determine. The newcomers again pushed down some of the fallen rocks, which had accumulated to a depth of over two feet since the first residents had moved out. These people must have been a large group for they occupied nearly all of the shelter whereas the former people had only utilized about one-third of the available space.

Again a death occurred among the children and burial was made near the back wall at the other end of the shelter. Probably both people had aided the natural efficiency of the shelter by leaning poles against the face of the cliff and covering them with skins. In these semi-lighted shelters such things as arrowpoints, bone awls, a harpoon and a bone fishhook fell unnoticed to join the growing accumulation of animal bones, ashes, flint chips and pieces of broken pottery jars which covered the uneven rocky floor.

Not far away was found the mute evidence that a woman, probably a captive, had been eaten and the broken and split bones of her body buried in a pile with her head placed atop the heap. Sometime after this cannibalistic event, the group moved on and the shelter again became the winter hiding place of rattlesnakes and deserted until our arrival except for occasional soldiers and hunters who perhaps used it as a refuge from storms.

Another important piece of evidence of our state's former inhabitants came to light on the Jesse Rivers' farm near Vergennes. Here beneath a gently rolling pasture formed by the junction of the Dead and Otter Creeks, we found the vestiges of a large Indian village. This is known locally as "Shanty Point" although no one could be found who remembered hearing that a building had ever stood on this spot. However, in the first section excavated, the topsoil yielded such semi-modern objects as brass cuff links, a two-tined iron fork, folding jackknife, white clay pipe fragments, an iron knife with bone handle, bone and silver plated buttons and many nails. All of these probably came from the hut of an early settler which might have stood here during the eighteenth century.

Six square areas, twenty feet on a side, were thoroughly examined during the season, June to October, and a wealth of archeological material recovered. The depth of each object and its relation to the corner stakes of the section were noted. Photographs were taken of certain objects in situ and many sketches were made so that as complete a picture as possible could be obtained of these people. Indian artifacts

Supposed Indian mortar, Athens, Vermont. Dimensions about
21 inches in diameter, 6½ inches deep; on side of boulder
6 x 4 feet.

Rock shelter at
Chipman's Point, Vermont

were found at all depths ranging from the plow soil to three feet in the yellow sand which underlay the dark humus mantle covering all of the sections examined. Thirty-nine pits were opened, all of which extended from the black topsoil down into the yellow sand and, since they had been filled with Indian refuse, were easily discernible. Some were cooking pits and were filled with fire-cracked stones while others had probably been corn storage pits. Later when the corn had been consumed they were filled with camp debris. The majority of our specimens came from these pits.

Let us examine the contents of several of the more interesting pits.

On the very bottom of one pit was found a small pile of objects consisting of a sinewstone or abrading stone and an undrilled oval slate pendant upon which were placed two bear canine teeth, one incisor tooth of both the beaver and the porcupine, a shark-like fish tooth, five triangular chert arrowpoints, five oval scrapers, one perforator, and a broken bone needle. This cache of objects may have been made as an offering to the spirit of the bear, some of whose bones were included in the group.

A nearby pit yielded, in several hundred fragments, the pottery jar illustrated above in restored condition. Practically all the jar was found along the bottom of the pit where it must have been broken when thrown, for most of the pieces which fit together lay beside each other. Note the rounded bottom and body of the jar with constricted neck and overhanging collar surmounted with four castellations or points. Ten holes were drilled through the jar, evidently in an attempt to repair a crack by tying. The collar has been decorated with triangular plats filled with incised parallel lines and also rows of lines parallel to the lip. From this type of decoration and the shape of the jar, we conclude that it is a product of an Iroquoian Indian although nearly all the other evidence from this place shows an occupation by an Algonkin speaking stock. Most of the other pottery fragments encountered have been non-Iroquoian.

Two more pottery jars were found side by side in another pit. They had been placed mouth down and were probably intact when buried, although the weight of the earth and frost had shattered them badly since they had not been made of as good grade of clay as the one illustrated. They appear to be the work of an Algonkin potter and we hope to have them restored in the near future.

One pit proved of special interest because of the quantity of bone implements found within. Implements of bone from Vermont have hitherto been almost nonexistent. One singular discovery was that of a bone fishhook cut from a piece of mammal leg bone. The point lacks a barb, as do most prehistoric Indian hooks, although the shaft is knobbed to facilitate fastening the line. Another form of hook coming from this pit was a slender double pointed shaft of bone known as a gorge. By tying in the middle this became lodged across the fish's throat when the line was pulled. A small slender bone tube with one end carbonized was found. It may have been used as a stem for a stone pipe bowl, which would account for the charred end. Other bone implements found consisted of awls, knives and arrowpoints with hollow bases for insertion of the arrow shaft.

The other implements recovered from the various pits consisted of notched, stemmed, and triangular arrowpoints, of quartzite, chert, and jasper; knives of the same materials; scrapers, usually oval in shape; perforators; notched axes; one holed pendent; a bannerstone fragment and many hammerstones. Along with hundreds of pottery fragments, we collected several crude pottery pipe stems.

During our excavations we uncovered four burials. All had been made in fairly shallow refuse pits, indeed one was so shallow that the plow had destroyed most of the skeleton. Of another body, nothing was discernible except a badly decayed skull. The remaining two were found buried together in a shallow rubbish pit and were in a fair state of preservation. The bones were carefully removed and a restoration of this double burial will soon be placed on display in the Robert Hull Fleming Museum of the University of Vermont.

All the material collected during the field season of 1938 has been brought to the Fleming Museum for the winter where it is being cleaned, restored, cataloged, photographed and studied. Certain of the more outstanding specimens will be placed on display from time to time so that modern Vermonters may have an opportunity of studying the implements and utensils of the ancient inhabitants of our land.

Persons desiring to cooperate in carrying on this worthy project in the writing of an otherwise unwritten history, may obtain suggestions and information from the Museum.

EXCERPTS FROM

Bulletin of the Champlain Valley
Archaeological Society, Vol. I, June 1939, No. 2

A GROUND SLATE PRODUCING SITE NEAR VERGENNES, VERMONT
by
John H. Bailey, Archaeologist

(No plates available)

For many years, every comprehensive paper or book dealing
with the archaeology of the northeast contained some reference
to the Eskimo-like culture which was found scattered sporadi-
cally over the area. Slate implements have been picked up here
and there in the form of lance or projectile points and ulus
or semilunar shaped knives, all with ground edges. Some of the
early investigators, namely Dr. C. C. Abbott[1] and Rev. W. M.
Beauchamp[2], first called attention to the similarity of these
tools with those in use by fairly recent Eskimoan people. However, nothing could be said with any degree of certainty concerning what other traits were associated with the ground slate
implements since all known specimens had been found in plowed
fields or wash-outs. For this reason, some of the early students were prone to expound quite elaborate theories concerning the presence of Eskimo people as far south as New York and
New England. As more of these specimens came to light, often
from the same fields which had produced other artifacts,
recent archaeologists were able to make studied guesses as to
what traits would complete the cultural picture when a true
station of these people should be found.

Willoughby[3] places these tools in his pre-Algonquian
group along with such traits as the bannerstone, bayonet slate
point, plummet, gouge, and adze in a non-agricultural and non-
ceramic economy. Parker[4] attributes them to an Eskimo-like
culture associated with soapstone, but not clay pottery; chert
arrowpoints of broad and large form with sloping shoulders, as
well as lozenge-shaped; scrapers and perforators of chert;
celts; and from some of these possible Eskimo-like sites,
double pointed bilaterally barbed harpoons, gouges, and hemi-
spheres of hematite. From his investigations, he concludes
that these are the remains of a people influenced by the
Eskimo from the northeast or of the Eskimo themselves, the
former more probable. Wintemberg[5] in his description of these
implements reports sites which yielded Algonkian pottery as
well as the ground slate tools, but in all cases as surface
finds. The late George H. Perkins[6], pioneer archaeologist of
the Champlain Valley, recalls other students using these slate
points as evidence of an Eskimo migration to this region, but
doubts that the presence of slate implements will prove con-
vincing evidence to support this theory.

Such was more or less the picture of the ground slate Eskimo-like people in August 1937 when the Champlain Valley Archaeological Society moved a party to the John Donovan farm at the junction of the Dead and Otter Creeks in the Township of Ferrisburg about four miles from Vergennes, Vermont. The Society wishes to express its appreciation to Mr. and Mrs. John Donovan for such cooperation as they were able to give. The excavating was carried on through the generous financial aid of Mr. H. Jermain Slocum, President of the Society, under the direction of the writer and supervised by Mr. William A. Ross of St. Albans, Vermont; assisted by David Chase and William Dorn, both of Rochester, New York; Henry Smith of Vergennes and George Elliott of Bristol, Vermont. To each of them, the writer takes this opportunity of expressing his gratitude for their enthusiastic cooperation. The presence of the site had been brought to the attention of the Society by Mr. Ross who had collected surface artifacts from the adjoining fields for many years.

The area examined was situated upon a long, gently sloping, tongue of land which terminated in Dead Creek and whose axis extended in a north-west, south-east direction. The site lay in a narrow strip of pasture land which, fortunately for the investigators, had never been plowed, bordered by Dead Creek on the south-east side and bounded on the north-west by a fence line and plowed field from which many artifacts had been taken in past years. A roughly rectangular area fifty feet wide and one hundred and fifty feet long extending along the ridge was thoroughly examined during the ensuing months of August, September, and October.

Previous testing had located the deepest and richest part of the deposit along the top of the ridge and this area was staked off into sections ten feet on a side and a combined numerical and alphabetical symbol given each section for designation and reference. It was at first believed that we had a site of a pit making people and that the majority of our specimens would come from pits. Several of our test holes disclosed what appeared to be pits which produced a considerable quantity of broken pottery. For this reason the sod was stripped from several sections exposing oval areas of discolored soil, but subsequent investigation revealed very little artificial material with the exception of chips in these depressions. In fact, the only two depressions which did produce any quantity of specimens were those which our test holes had located. Since it now appeared that our artifacts were going to be found in the scant refuse mantle and not in the so-called pits, we changed our methods and specialized upon the sod and shallow refuse.

As our excavating progressed, it became apparent that we were dealing with a homogeneous refuse mantle of black sandy loam resting upon an uneven sand-clay subsoil. In certain sections the subsoil presented such irregularities of level that it was impossible to determine the outline of anything resembling an aboriginal excavation. The average definable depression was represented by a long oval subsoil concavity ranging in length from five to ten feet and in breadth from two to five feet with depths varying from fifteen to forty inches. All of these had gently sloping sides with almost pointed bottoms and never extended into the topsoil, as far as could be determined. Whether or not they were actual dug pits is highly problematical. For the majority of them, a more reasonable solution of their origin might be that they were formed either by prehistoric tree falls or by erosion with the resulting depressions filled with debris. However, one interesting arrangement which could not have been the result of natural agencies was a shallow trapezoidal shaped pit with a circular one twelve inches in diameter located six inches outside the center of its base.

Several of the oval pits contained quantities of pottery fragments, usually within a few inches of the bottom and in one case the pottery was four or five layers deep and for the larger part in very friable condition. In only one of the so-called pits was stratification discernible. This pit was roughly semicircular with gently sloping sides on the circumference and a steep slope on the diameter side. The pit reached a depth of 40 1/2 inches, the maximum for any of the pits and depressions and presented a singular stratification for this site. It consisted of a bottom layer of black greasy soil with a central thickness of four inches overlaid by a five inch layer of sterile clay. This, in turn, was overburdened by a thin layer of white ash-like substance blending upward into a black sandy clay composition with a central thickness of eleven and one-half inches. Above this was a twelve inch layer of clay loam containing a few chips of chert and quartzite and some charcoal flakes, while the remaining eight inches contained the normal refuse mantle and sod line. Several of the other pits showed evidence in their peripheral regions that sometime while open, portions of the clay walls had slipped into the pit burying under sterile clay marginal sections of the black refuse deposit then lying on the bottom. Some of the layers in the previously described pit may owe their existence to similar phenomena occurring over a longer period of time or during a particularly rainy season.

No discernable evidence was uncovered which would give us a clue to the shape of the dwelling used by these people. However, on the bottom of one of the large irregular shaped depressions was uncovered a hearth. Here arranged in a semicircle were five large limestone slabs with several smaller ones between while the central area, about twenty-four inches in diameter, contained charcoal, fragments of burned bone, and quartzite chips. Three feet from the open side was discovered a post-mould five inches in diameter and extending about ten inches into the subsoil. The post-mould entered the ground at such an angle that an implanted post would have extended over the hearth. An analogous arrangement is reported by Cole and Deuel from Fulton County, Illinois.

- 9 -

By inserting a green post, it would have made a very convenient device for suspending roasting meat over the fire. Let us assume the above theory to be correct. Since the hearth was found at a depth of twenty-one inches in one of the largest depressions uncovered, we may have here the floor of a semi-subterranean dwelling. It does not seem likely that they would have excavated such a large area, roughly ten by eleven feet, for cooking purposes only. The large rocks must have been brought in for they are non-indigenous in the subsoil.

No implements of bone and only a few badly decayed pieces of refuse bone and many calcined chips were encountered. In the hope of discovering why bone was so poorly preserved, samples of the soil were submitted for examination to Professor A. F. Gustafson of Cornell University, Ithaca, New York in order that the degree of acidity of the soil might be determined. It was found to have a pH of 5.69 or a highly acid content. At the same time were submitted samples of the soil from a site just across Dead Creek which produced many bone implements and much refuse bone from both the pits and the topsoil debris. The report on these samples was a pH of 7.40 or a basic condition. Whether this is the complete solution, namely that the acid soil had dissolved most of the bone, we cannot say and until similar situations[8] have been found and tested, our hypothesis must remain tentative. In one section we did encounter refuse bone in well preserved condition. However, as we progressed we uncovered a large pit containing layers of white ash surrounding large fire cracked and stained rocks. From this pit we removed such semi-modern objects as gunflints, white clay pipe bowls and stems, musket balls, a handle from a pewter spoon, scraps of sheet brass, an iron awl, copper finger ring, silver-plated button, two hollow brass buttons, and a miniature axe made by cutting a scrap of brass to shape and riveting it around a wooden handle, a portion of which still remained. There was also a complete skeleton of a turtle, a bone awl six and one-half inches long, and a deer phalangeal bone cut, but not drilled. Here in this combined refuse and cooking pit of a small group of Indians of about 1750, we found our source of the well preserved bone and, if conditions have remained constant, one may comprehend the antiquity of the first dwellers upon this spot, most of whose refuse bones had vanished without leaving more than a trace.

Over six thousand square feet of the pasture were thoroughly examined, with the resultant collection of over seven hundred nearly complete specimens plus many more fragments of pottery, rejects, and broken artifacts. The majority of these specimens came from the shallow refuse mantle and most of them from depths ranging from two to twelve inches. In order to facilitate our study of these specimens, let us consider then under the divisions of ground and polished stone, rough stone, chipped stone, and pottery, leaving the discussion of cultural relationship to a later portion of this paper.

Ground and Polished Stone.

Of prime importance in this group are the nine fragments
of ground slate semilunar knives or ulus and the one broad
bladed point of like material. The ulus are all of slate,
varying in color from light tan to dark gray and several were
made from banded material. Our largest example was found in
seven fragments over an area roughly four feet in diameter and
at a uniform depth of eight inches. In its original form it
must have had a length of over 6 1/2 inches and a breadth of
3 1/2 inches. It has a surface ground smooth along the handle
edge. While two of the fragments may have had this smooth
handle edge originally, no evidence now remains for they were
evidently chipped along the entire portion present. However
they may never have been finished. None of our fragments show
any evidence of a perforation for the attachment of a wooden
handle and only one has a slight remnant of a ridge-like handle
which suggests Willoughby's[9] monolithic form. It is a flat,
thin, badly shattered fragment with one surface terminating in
the lower edge of a straight ridge across the top of the specimen. This may be the remnant of a handle. One fragment is
from along the cutting edge and it is difficult to say what
form of handle surface it possessed. All of these knife specimens have the cutting edge ground sharp. A small end portion
of one was found which had been ground to shape and then chipped, perhaps in preparation for the final grinding which would
result in the cutting edge. Our one broad bladed point or
lance head is made from dull reddish slate whose source may
have been an outcropping near Granville, Washington County,
New York.[10] Both the tip and the base ends have been broken
off, but enough remains at the basal end to show portions of
the ground notches so common in this type of implement. All
of these ground slate implements were found at depths ranging
from three to nine inches with the majority coming from the
five to eight inch level. In every case at least three inches
of refuse earth separated them from the subsoil.

Another singular discovery is a broken rectangular fragment of black slate ground with two parallel edges and broken
at both ends. It has been ground in a beveled manner so that
it is hexagonal in cross section with but one edge sharp. It
may very well be a section from a bayonet slate knife or dagger
similar to ones reported by Willoughby[11] and Moorehead[12] from
the "Red Paint graves" of Maine. It was found at a depth of
ten inches in one of the pits along with several pieces of
undecorated pottery.

The fragment of a semicircular object is probably part of
a bannerstone. It is made of a thin piece of schist with two
original ground edges and is decorated on one surface by short
parallel dashes perpendicular to them. It is probably the
wing of a bipennate form of bannerstone although unfortunately
no evidence of the type of central septum remains on our
specimen.

The only artifact indicating drilling is roughly trape-zoidal in shape and bears the portions of two drill holes near the base, breaks having occurred through both of them. It is made from tan steatite and is highly polished upon all sur-faces except for a small section on the basal side between the two perforations which has been slightly smoothed. A possible explanation is that the holes were drilled in an attempt to repair a highly coveted object. Unfortunately only this portion of the specimen was recovered so that we cannot say just what shape the perfect object might have taken.

The remaining fragments of ground and polished problem-atical forms consist of a rectangular slate fragment with ground notches, possibly the base of a crude slate arrowpoint, and three polished rectangular position of slate objects. Two of these may be wing fragments of bannerstones, but another, being less than one inch in breadth, could not be explained in this way because of its size.

In the range of large cutting tools we have three complete crude gouges. All are of the short, broad, shallow groove type and exhibit polishing along the cutting edge only. Indeed, one of them has its concave surface covered with "peck marks" and may never have been finished. All are concavo-convex in cross section and are relatively crude in comparison with a small bit fragment with is from a well made gouge of schist with a shallow groove and flaring edge. A section of a thick, narrow gouge bears a portion of the medial end of the groove. Two other fragments of gouges in process of manufacture were recovered from the refuse mantle.

Small cutting tools are represented by one small triangu-loid celt of green serpentine and a thin bit portion of another of tan porphyry. A thin adze or celt, badly battered, has a slight shallow notch on one side and the other straight with both poll and bit ends shattered by use. We also have a thin adze-like scraper of dark slate with only the cutting edge ground. Several other bit fragments of adzes and the poll end of either a celt or adze were collected.

Rough Stone

The range of forms within this subdivision is not very large since it consists primarily of sinewstones, hammerstones, and whetstones.

Our two specimens may be provisionally called sinewstones or abrading stones. The larger example is made from a pinkish quartzite, egg shaped, waterworn pebble, the large end of which has been about half worn away by a broad uneven groove. At the smaller end and upon the opposite side is a single deep narrow groove approximately in the center. The other specimen is a fragment exhibiting one broad shallow groove upon each edge and evidence of battering along the circumference between. Whether these implements were used for fashioning from deer sinew the strings for the Indian bow or for sharpening their celts and adzes, we cannot tell.

The hammerstones may be tentatively grouped into three divisions and in all cases are unpitted. The most prevalent form occurring here was a circular or oval, relatively thick, block of quartzite bearing evidence of use as a hammer sometimes on the ends, one or both, and less often along the whole circumference. Of the 62 hammerstones recovered, 32 fall into this group. The second division consists of a natural pebble of quartzite or granite battered in the same manner as the block type. Only six examples of this form were found. Representatives of the third grouping are thin, usually circular, chipped disks with some battering upon their periphery. Twenty-four specimens of this type were recovered. Chert was used in making only four of the hammerstones found. It is fabricated from a chipped spall of mottled dark tan and black chert with a well hammered point upon each end.

The apparent grinding on several fragments of roughly worked limestone, sandstone, and schist has lead us to believe that these might have been used as whetstones or grinding stones in fashioning and sharpening stone implements. The specimens are rectangular, circular, and oval in cross section. The rectangular one exhibits a decided twist of the surfaces toward one end. The only complete specimen is a slender one of schist with beveled edges, doubtless the result of much rubbing The others in this group show some evidence of abrasive use along the sides and edges. Another form encountered consists of a flat oval pebble with its surfaces worn slightly concave, apparently by grinding. Six fragments of these are found. They were probably held in the hand since all are relatively small.

Chipped Stone

It is in this class that we find our greatest diversity of form and also the majority of our specimens. In this group are found the numerous projectile points, arrow, javelin, and spear; knives; scrapers; perforators; and aberrant forms.

In order to simplify our discussion of projectile point types we have considered them in groups differentiated by their geometrical forms which may be readily recognized. First in preponderance of numbers represented come the triangular arrowpoints. Over 55% of the 570 points recovered were triangular in shape. They range in length for finished examples, from 3/4 of an inch to 2 inches. An overwhelming majority of the triangular points, both in the chert and quartzite medium, have concave bases and are equilateral triangles. A very small number, evenly divided in material between chert and quartzite, have almost straight bases and eight have round or oval bases. Many of our triangular rejects are too crudely flaked to be considered finished products, but may have been intended for triangular points.

In our study of the triangular points, we found a few which appeared to be plain triangles, but upon closer examination a slight notching near the corners was noted. We have provisionally called these "notched triangles." In all, thirteen of this form were separated from the normal triangles and of these, three were of quartzite and the rest of chert. Most of them are of medium length, averaging 1 1/8 inches.

Next, in simplicity of shape, are the stemmed projectile points. Most of these have a straight or parallel sided stem broadening out into the base of the blade. Nearly all of them are long, slender heads. They vary in length from 1 1/8" to 2 5/8" and of the thirty-seven points fitting into this class, twenty-three are of chert, usually of a dark hue, while the remainder are of quartzite, barring one, which is of smoky quartz. The quartzite specimens exhibit a poorer grade of workmanship than the chert specimens, but this is doubtless due to the nature of the material used.

We now come to a group which is rather difficult to differentiate from other types. These might be called corner notched to separate them from the very similar side notched form. In order to clarify our terminology, let us define a corner notched point as one with a definite notch in or near the corner and with a width of base less than the width of blade immediately above the notch. With this in mind, let us turn to a consideration of the sixty-five projectile points which fit this definition. They vary in length from 3/4" to 2 1/4" and are about equally divided between chert and quartzite with several examples made from slate. Many, in both major materials, have notches sloping upward toward the tip. Those with concave bases are predominant, with a good share having the edge of the concavity rubbed or ground smooth.

Our next subdivision may be called side notched points which differ from the corner notched in having the notch some distance up from the corner and the base as wide or wider than the blade. They vary in length from 1" to 2 1/8" with an average length for the 49 points of about 1 3/4". Again they are about equally divided between chert and quartzite although eight of the specimens are made of slate or argillite. As in the case of the corner notched form, the majority of the quartzite points have a concave basal edge rounded smooth. Many of our examples have a deep rectangular shaped notch while others show a shallow concave notching.

The "eared" side notched points, of the type recently described by Ritchie[13] for the Laurentian Aspect, are represented by four examples which closely approximate this shape. Two of them consist of a notched point with a wide base which extends beyond the edge of the blade and forms a tang or "ear." Two of our specimens are made of chert, the others of quartzite, all having a concave basal edge.

We come now to the javelin and spear head group and are again confronted with the problem of how to distinguish between a large arrowpoint and a short javelin head. In our separation of types, we have taken as criteria the length, breadth, thickness, and weight of the point. All the examples we have provisionally called javelin and spear points seemed either too long, broad, or heavy to have tipped an arrow without handicapping its range and efficiency. Of the fifty-two perfect and fragmentary specimens forming this group, thirty are of quartzite and almost all have rubbed bases. The remaining 22 examples are of varying hues of chert with two of slate or argillite. Nearly all, both of chert and quartzite but for their size would fall into our side notched category for arrowpoints.

Many of our knives are similar in shape to the notched arrowpoints, differing from them only in being asymmetrical, that is having one edge of the blade fairly straight and shorter than the other, which usually is made with a definite curve. One large notched implement is too blunt to have been a javelin or spear head although resembling one in shape, and since one edge is sharp and well chipped while the other is rough and irregular, it was probably used as a knife.

A considerable number of scrapers, ninety-four in all, was recovered and present a variety of shapes. Almost half of these specimens show evidence of a marginal retouching along one edge or side of the flakes which vary in thickness from 1/8 to 1/2 inch and which have no uniformity of shape. Several of these are ridged or "keeled" with the thickest portion near the cutting edge. Over two-thirds of them have been made from chert, usually of dark hue.

Our next most common form of scraper, an oval flake with marginal retouching around most of its circumference is usually thin and of the twenty-seven fitting into this class, only six are of quartzite and the rest of chert. The few remaining scrapers, with four exceptions are triangular with the scraper edges at the convex bases. Some of these may have been reworked from the tips of broken arrowpoints and some have thick, well polished bases. Only one corner notched scraper was located and it is made of dark gray chert. A unique form of scraper consists of a flake with two parallel cutting edges and a concave under-surface, while two others have parallel cutting edges.

We come now to our last definite group of chipped implements, namely, the perforators or drills. The prevalent form appears to be the expanded base type with a long and slender drill point. Ranging in length from 1 1/2" to 2 1/2" for complete specimens, all, except three, of the twenty-one examples are of chert. Another equally common shape is triangular with concave sides converging to form a point. It is represented by twenty-three specimens. Most of them have been fabricated of chert. A third type we have chosen to call "T"

- 15 -

shaped because of its resemblance to the letter T. All are of chert and bear short, broad, drill points. A closely related form has a deep concave base, but is very similar in shape and size. Of the variety common to the Champlain Valley, the side or corner notched type, we have but three examples; one other might fit this classification, although it appears to have been an arrowpoint partially transformed into a perforator. One other quartzite fragment also shows this practice. Two perforators, singular in shape, were found. One is a double pointed drill while the other is a well made drill point on a fluke, a form quite characteristic of the Owasco Aspect. Another peculiar shape appears to have had originally a diamond shaped base. All three are of chert.

There are a few aberrant forms which do not fit any of our defined chipped types. One is a curved, chert object showing secondary chipping along the edges, but unfortunately broken at one end so that it is impossible even to hazard a guess as to its use. The other is also of chert with one long and one short tang, but again broken on one side.

We must not leave our discussion of the chipped stone artifacts without reference to the numerous fragments of roughly chipped blades which were recovered. Several hundred base and point fragments were found. Judging from the similarity of shape and material of these fragments to some found on a quarry site near Bristol, Vermont, about eight miles east of this site, we have concluded these could have been quarry blanks which were roughed out by percussion at the quarry and brought back to the permanent habitation to be finished into tools.

Pottery

Fragments of pottery were recovered from all sections and all depths of the refuse deposit and from two of the pit-like depressions. As far as could be determined there was no correlation of any type of ware against depth and pieces from one section often fitted together with sherds from others twenty or thirty feet away. All sherds are grit tempered, crystalline fragments of quartz, schist, mica and feldspar having been identified from certain of the sherds.   The size of the aplastic ranges from crystals 1/4 of an inch on a side to small ones the size of a pinhead. The hardness[14] of the ware is within the range 2.0 to 3.5, with a predominant number of the sherds showing a hardness of 2.0-2.5. The texture of the paste varies from coarse to medium coarse with a majority of the fragments having a medium coarse texture. In the largest percentage of our sherds, the temper constituted one-third or less of the paste. The fragments vary in thickness from 1/4 of an inch to 3/4 of an inch for body sherds and average about 3/8 of an inch. The average for rim fragments is slightly less. Most of our sherds have smoke blackened interior surfaces and in several cases have definite layers of carbonized food. Fewer have their exterior surfaces smoke blacked. In color, the pottery includes various shades of dull red, tan, and dark gray. However, the reds and tans predominate.

Among the more than siz hundred pottery fragments recovered approximately one hundred and fifty may be called rim fragments, that is, ones bearing an identifiable portion of the lip. In turn, these rim sherds represent at least 64 different jars. This should give some idea of the number of potters at work or the time involved in the occupation of the site. Eleven of the jars show narrow collars, six of which were made by applying a thin strip of clay before firing.

The most common form of decorative motif.appears to have been made by applying a cord or fiber wound twig to the damp clay, making impressions of various lengths which meet the lip at all angles. Often combined with the above is a row of round impressions, encircling the jar a short distance below the rim, apparently made by a hollow reed-like instrument which leaves a convex surface at the bottom of the annular impression, and in many examples bulges the clay on the interior surface. This decorative design anpears on both collared and non-collared jars and in combination with other than cord wrapped twig impressions. One has broad, shallow, parallel lines drawn perpendicularly downward from the lip edge. The other has similar broad, shallow lines drawn roughly perpendicular and parallel to the lip making a rectangular lattice work design. Several body sherds, probably from these same jars since they exhibit a similar design, color, and texture were found. In one example the circular impression motif appears on an otherwise entirely plain rim fragment. Several rim fragments exhibit short parallel lines incised with a blunt stylus and making an acute angle with the lip edge. Another jar is represented by only one fragment and is decorated by broad parallel lines applied by impressing a notched twig or some other sectional object. The lip is overhanging, slopes outward and is decorated, as is the interior for about an inch below it. Another small rim fragment shows rows of impressions made by a chisel-like instrument parallel to the lip. One rim sherd and several other fragments were found which are decorated by two sets of deep narrow incised lines crossing each other acutely and forming a diamond design. In the rim fragment, the lip is narrow and rounded.

Some of the body sherds were plain, but more bore some form of intentional design or one due to some process in the manufacture of the jar such as "paddling." Since many of the sherds are from near the rim, the most common design form found is the cord wound twig impression. One type appears to have been impressed with a crude fabric and is represented by eight definite examples and 55 possible ones which may be cord wound paddle marked. Several specimens show incised parallel lines which may have been made by a three toothed stick or "comb."

In the range of lip forms, we find both round and flat, broad and narrow, and decorated and undecorated. One of the pits produced about one-third of the rim of a jar with a thickened lower edge which narrows up to a rounded lip. The

lip and rim are decorated with cord impressions and the interior surface bears broad incised lines or channeling. Most
of the lip surfaces are out-sloping.

Our pottery jar is restored from fragments found in one
of the pits which also contained other sherds. However, a
group of sherds found about fifteen feet away, resting almost
on the subsoil, and fragments from other sections were part
of this jar and helped substantially in the restoration of the
bottom and part of one side. The wide spread scattering of
this jar would indicate that the material taken from within
this area belongs to one group. The slightly pointed, constricted bottom and parts of one side are original. Portions
of the rim, also original, are probably from the same jar
since in texture, color and decoration they are similar to the
body, although there is no place where they actually tie together. The jar is made from a hard, thin, reddish pottery,
easily distinguishable from fragments of a coarse friable jar
represented by rim fragments and pieces of its constricted
conoidal bottom which were found in the same pit. Our restored jar has a comparatively plain body surface bearing only
broad shallow lines apparently applied at random since they
cross each other at all angles. The body is constricted toward the rim forming a narrow mouthed jar. The lip is plain,
narrow, rounded, and undecorated. About an inch below it
there is a row of circular impressions bulging the clay on
the inside. Below these, at a varying distance, are four rows
of small circular impressions made by a bluntly pointed instrument and over these in some areas are the long random scratch
marks, also found on the body portion of the jar.

Many of our pottery sherds exhibit fairly straight breaks
with either convex or concave smooth edge surfaces. This
evidence combined with at least six cylindrical clay coil
portions, perhaps accidently fired, gives us fairly conclusive proof that a good portion of our pottery was made by
the coiling method. The restored pottery jar contained many
sherds which had broken along the coils giving further
evidence to substantiate this belief.

Four sherds of relatively thin steatite or soapstone
vessels were found. Three are plain body fragments, but one
is a rim sherd having narrow notches cut across the lip. No
evidence of a handle remains.

Conclusions

We believe that in the Donovan location we have a closed
site or one occupied by only one people. A plotting of speci
mens against depth for various sections revealed that all of
the various types of projectile points covered the same range
of depths. The pottery came anywhere from just below the sod
line to the subsoil and no differentiation of pottery type at
various depths could be determined. Scrapers and perforators
appear to be clustered between the depths of three and nine

inches, but with a usual maximum artifact depth of one foot, this apparent grouping cannot be given very much significance. The ground slate implements are definitely a part of the complex. In practically all instances of their discovery, notched and triangular arrowpoints and pottery occurred within a few feet of them, and at the same level, as well as above and below them. Nor were they localized in any one section or group of sections, but were found in widely separated portions of the excavated area. In case we have the remains of a small group of people living and moving about for a considerable period of time within a rather localized area, the scattered fragments must prove that the ground slates were a part of the complex during the entire occupation of the site. The discovery of seven pieces of the same knife within a radius of three feet should discredit any theory claiming their subsequent introduction by either human or natural agencies into an earlier occupation mantle.

We here have a small village site of a non-agricultural, semi-sedentary people who existed by hunting and fishing since none of their implements can be construed as having been employed in the cultivation and preparation of corn. They were assuredly potters making a simple pointed bottomed jar, decorated with cord wound twig and circular impressions. They also used a few steatite vessels. Hunting was carried on by the bow and arrow tipped with a wide variety of point types, the javelin, and the spear. Presumably they traveled in dugout canoes in whose manufacture the gouges were employed. They were the first recorded users for our area of the ground slate semilunar knife and lance head. Since no pipes were found, we may safely assume that they did not use or raise tobacco. In ceremonial traits, only the bannerstone's use is suggested by several wing fragments. However, the pendant or gorget may have been worn, since one fragment of what may have been a gorget with two drill holes did occur[15]. Nothing can be reported concerning the bone component of this complex or the skeletal type of the inhabitants since neither bone implements were recovered nor was the burial ground located. From the cultural traits present, we believe that we have a manifestation of an eastern Woodland people, possibly of Algonkin stock.

In the same summer the Rochester Museum of Arts and Sciences excavated, under the supervision of William A. Ritchie[16], two village sites on opposite banks of the Oneida River at Brewerton just as it emerges from Oneida Lake in Central New York. A comparison of the artifacts from these two sites with those obtained on the Donovan farm showed a remarkable similarity in many respects. Brewerton produced the same wide variety of projectile points; the same scrapers, although the notched form was more prevalent; and practically the same types of perforators. In the group of rough stone implements at Brewerton were found crude choppers, net-sinkers, unpitted hammerstones, anvilstones, cylindrical and conical pestles, mullers, metates, whetstones, a plummet, and a

partially grooved oval stone. Vergennes produced only two of
these rough stone types; the hammerstone and the whetstone,
and the additional trait of the sinewstone. Polished stone
artifacts from Brewerton included the gouge of both short-broad
and long-narrow form, the bannerstone, celt, and piano-convex
adze. The Donovan farm has all of these traits plus the ground
slate ulu and point, while one of the Brewerton stations produced as a surface find a slate point. The New York and
Vermont components have pottery of similar texture, color,
shape, and decoration and while pottery came from all depths
at Vergennes, it was almost entirely confined to the upper
half of the deep Brewerton deposits. One of the Brewerton
stations produced the bone implements for this culture and
both yielded various forms of native copper implements, all of
which were lacking at Vergennes.

The occurrence of a majority of these traits at both
Brewerton and Vergennes and the marked similarity of the
pottery at both places has lead to the conclusion that we are
dealing with essentially the same culture. Various surface
sites in the Hudson-Mohawk region of New York have also produced similar artifacts which suggest a valid connection for
these sites with this new culture for the northeast. The
presence of a section of a bayonet slate knife at Vergennes
hints at some association with the "Red Paint" people of Maine.

The new result of the combination of the work at Brewerton,
Vergennes, and in the Hudson-Mohawk region has been the defin-
ing of a new culture which, in the terminology of the McKern
classificatory system, Parker and Ritchie have termed the
Laurentian Aspect and Ritchie[17] has already tentatively distinguished two foci: the Brewerton and Vosburg (the latter
from the Hudson-Mohawk sites) to which this work adds a possible third which the writer has chosen to call the Vergennes.
The differentiation of the foci has been made upon the presence
at certain stations and absence at others of the ground slate
implements, the plummet, native copper artifacts, and the
sinewstone. Common to all foci are the gouge, a wide variety
of projectile point types, scrapers, perforators, and pottery.

What clues do we have as to the origin of these people?
The similarity of the ground slate implements with Eskimo
tools was recognized long ago and suggests some connection
with the north. However, since many of our traits, as pottery,
the bannerstone, and gouge are non-Eskimoan, we cannot say that
we have a pure Eskimo culture, but merely one showing Eskimo
influence. A search of the literature has revealed an early
Eskimo culture reported by Jenness[18] and Wintemberg and tentatively named by them the Cape Dorset Eskimo culture. Unfortunately, not too much is known concerning this culture but what
is known came from sites on Cape Dorset in the southeastern
corner of Baffin Island, far in the Northland; and from
surface sites near Bradore Bay[19] on the eastern boundary of
Quebec and Labrador. From these sites have come semilunar
knives, notched and triangular arrowpoints of chert, scrapers,

narrow knife blades, and a steatite plummet. Other stone types
found are cylindrical hammerstones, adze blades, and a sandstone lamp. The bone implement component is largely Eskimoan
with harpoonheads having rectangular sockets, bone knife
handles, needles with gouged out eyelets, and bone objects,
probably charms or ornaments.

Strong[20] reports three small sites on or near the coast
of northeastern Labrador which he believes may have some
cultural connection with the Cape Dorset people. These sites
produced, largely as surface finds, notched, stemmed, and triangular arrowpoints, crude semilunar knives, a gouge, adzes,
whetstones, hammerstones, and a triangular pendant with gouged holes. No pottery and only a few calcined chips of bone
were obtained from these stations. Strong believes that "we
have in northeastern North America a widespread early archaeological horizon which contains nearly all the basic elements
essential to the development of both Indian and Eskimo
cultures as they appear in historic times."

Speck[21] and Wintemberg[22] tell of a large surface site at
Tadoussac on the north shore of the St. Lawrence at the mouth
of the Saguenay River from which have been recovered leaf and
lozenge shaped arrowpoints, plane-like scrapers, semilunar
knives, long and slender ground slate points, gouges, adzes,
chisels, plummets, whetstones, and hammerstones. Although no
pottery was found here, it seems from those traits listed to
be another manifestation of our Laurentian culture.

The Dorset culture seems to be an Eskimoan manifestation
with definite Indian influence, as suggested by Jenness[23],
while our Laurentian people must be Indian with an Eskimoan
influence. If, as we now believe, they influenced each other,
they might have had a common source or contact ground some-
where in the Newfoundland-Labrador area. The Dorset people
worked northward leaving Wintemberg's and Strong's sites, the
Cape Dorset site itself, and others scattered over the Northland while the Laurentian people moved in a southwestern
direction up the St. Lawrence River Valley, pausing perhaps
for awhile at Tadoussac, and south into the Lake Champlain
and Lake Ontario regions where our key stations are located.
Many ground slate implements and Laurentian-like pottery have
been found all along the St. Lawrence River Valley.

However, further work must be done to the north before
this explanation may become anything but a very tentative
theory.

FOOTNOTES

1 Abbott, C. C. Primitive Industry, Salem, Mass., 1881,
     pp. 63-64.

2 Beauchamp, William M. Polished Stone Articles Used by the
     New York Aborigines, Bull. of N. Y. State Museum, Vol. 4,
     No. 18, Albany, 1897, pp. 65-72.

3   Willoughby, C. C.   Antiquities of the New England Indians,
        Peabody Museum, Harvard University, 1935, pp. 52-54, 70
        70-75.

4   Parker, Arthur C.   Archeological History of New York,
        Bull. of N. Y. State Museum, Nos. 235, 236, Albany, N. Y.,
        1926, pp. 79-83.

5   Wintemberg, W. J.   Distinguishing Characteristics of
        Algonkian and Irogquoian Cultures, Bull. No. 67,
        National Museum of Canada, 1929, pp. 70-71.

6   Perkins, George H.   Aboriginal Remains in the Champlain
        Balley, Am. Anth. n.s. Vol. 14, No. 1, 1912, pp. 79.

7   Cole and Deuel, Rediscovering Illinois, University of
        Chicago, Chicago, Illinois, 1937, p. 114.

8   An expedition of The Rochester Museum of Arts and Sciences
        under W. A. Ritchie found an analogous situation on
        opposite sides of the Oneida River at Brewerton, N. Y.,
        in 1937.

9   Willoughby, op. cit. p. 72.

10 Tentatively identified by Mr. Dan E. Edgerton of the
        Vermont Structural Slate Company of Fair Haven, Vermont.

11 Willoughby, Charles C.   Prehistoric Burial Places in
        Maine, Peabody Museum, Harvard University, Cambridge,
        Mass., Vol. 1, No. 6, 1898, p. 18.

12 Moorehead, Warren K.   A report on the Archaeology of
        Maine, Phillips Academy, Andover, Mass., 1922,
        pp. 121-123.

13 Ritchie, William A.   A Perspective of Northeastern
        Archaeology, American Antiquity, Vol. IV, No. 2, 1938,
        p. 107.

14 Tests made with Ceramic Hardness Standards of the
        University of Michigan, Museum of Anthropology.

15 Mr. Theodore Sherman of Fair Haven, Vermont, reports
        finding on this spot a broken one-holed pendant of
        slate. This has been included in the trait table at
        the end of this paper since it was found in the
        pasture and near our excavations.

16 Ritchie, William A.   A Perspective of Northeastern
        Archaeology, American Antiquity, Vol. IV, No. 2,
        October 1938, pp. 106-108; also Two Village Sites
        near Brewerton, N. Y., The Type Components of the
        Brewerton Focus, Laurentian Aspect, Research Records,
        No. 5, Rochester Museum of Arts and Sciences (In Press).

17   Ritchie, William A.   A Perspective of Northeastern
     Archaeology, American Antiquity, Vol. IV, No. 2,
     October 1938, pp. 106-108.

18   Jenness, Diamond.   Geographical Review, Vol. XV, No. 3,
     July 1925, pp. 428-437.   Also Problem of the Eskimo,
     The American Aborigines, Toronto, 1933, pp. 389-396.

19   Specimens from these sites examined through the courtesy
     of D. Jenness and W. J. Wintemberg at the National
     Museum of Canada, Ottawa.

20   Strong, William D.   A Stone Culture from Northern
     Labrador and Its Relation to the Eskimo-like Cultures
     of the Northeast, American Anthropologist, n.s.,
     Vol. 32, No. 1, 1930, pp. 126-144.

21   Speck, Frank G.   An Ancient Archaeological Site on the
     Lower St. Lawrence, Holmes Anniversary Volume,
     Washington, 1916, pp. 427-433.

22   Wintemberg, W. J.   Preliminary Report on Field Work in
     1927, Annual Report for 1927, Bulletin No. 56, National
     Museum of Canada, Ottawa, 1929, pp. 40-41.

23   Jenness, Diamond.   The Problem of the Eskimo, The
     American Aborigines, Toronto, 1933, p. 395.

A Laurentian Site in Addison County, Vermont.

(Interim Report, 1938-1951).

by Edward Brooks, Chairman
Archeological Committee
Vermont Historical Society

INTRODUCTION

At the confluence of Dead River with Otter Creek, in the Township of Ferrisburg, Addison County, Vermont, is a point of land that slopes gently northward from a higher plateau. This area, which is now in pasture, contains about five acres. A low ridge of land extends north and south along the center of this point which slopes gently to the banks of Dead River on the west and eastward to a small marsh which in turn is bounded by a State highway. On this point was once the site of an early Indian village.

In later days, it became the home of white settlers, and from this occupancy the area was known as "Shanty Point." Histories consulted do not record the dates of this occupancy, nor are there any living residents who remember any habitation or the names of those who made their homes upon that spot. Excavations by the late John H. Bailey uncovered a set of brass cuff links and English clay pipes, but no evidences of a dwelling were found.

"Shanty Point" has long been known to archeologists as containing the remains of aboriginal occupancy, but no intensive archeological investigations were carried on there until the Summer of 1938, when a portion of the site was explored by Mr. Bailey and the results of his findings published in a brief paper.[1]

During the Summer of 1946, the writer and Mr. Leaman F. Hallett of Mansfield, Massachusetts, excavated a small area at the northwest boundary of Bailey's operations and found a limestone-capped ash pit which contained a small pottery vessel. (Plate 12)

From June 15th to October 15th., 1951, further archeological explorations were carried on in this village site under the sponsorship of the Vermont Historical Society and the result of the work is the subject of this report.

It has long been our opinion that the Chronological Sequence for the State of New York, as prepared by Dr. William A. Ritchie, State Archeologist of that State,[2] is generally applicable for that portion of the Champlain Valley that lies within the western boundary of the State of Vermont. With this in view all pottery and chipped stone artifacts have been placed in their respective cultural sequences.

ACKNOWLEDGEMENTS

The writer expresses his warmest thanks to a leading Vermonter who has long been identified with constructive under-takings in the State, for the generous fund from which this undertaking was maintained. Also to Dr. William A. Ritchie, State Archeologist of the State of New York, for the type-ological and cultural classification of stone and pottery arti-facts, aid in the editing and preparation of this report and many other courtesies; to Dr. Arthur W. Peach, Director of the Vermont Historical Society and his entire Staff for their co-operation during the progress of the work; to Mr. E. K. Burnett, Asst., Director of the Museum of the American Indian, Heye Foundation for permission to use the photograph of the pottery vessel found previously on the site and now in the possession of the Museum; and to Mr. Charles E. Gillette, Senior Curator (Archeology) of the New York State Museum, for aid with photo-graphy. Professor Charles G. Doll, State Geologist of Vermont, who was most helpful with information on geological matters pertaining to the area, Hon. Wayland S. Bristol of Vergennes, Vt., and Mr. James Rivers, owner of the property, without whose permission this work could not have been carried out, also merit hearty thanks.

EXCAVATIONS OF 1951

A base line 300 feet long, running north and south, and 30 feet east of the high water mark of Dead River, was laid down on the western slope of the site. From each terminus of the base line, perpendicular lines were extended easterly 150 feet. The area thus staked out consisted of approximately 1.3 acres.

Starting easterly from the base line, a trench 75 feet long and 5 feet wide was excavated along the southern boundary of Bailey's excavations. This trench was measured off in 5 foot squares with stakes marking the corners of each square. The squares were each given a number and their stakes a com-bined numerical and alphabetical symbol for reference. The position of all artifacts recovered, as well as pits and post-molds were recorded with reference to the nearest stakes.

Rivers Farm (Excavation) Vergennes Vt.

Plate No. 1   View from air of the Rivers Site on the Otter Creek.   Excavation shown on point

Plate No. 2   View of the site, looking north east,
toward Otter Creek

Plate No. 3   The Beach looking south west up Dead River

Plate No. 4   Restored Iroquis pot from Rivers Site
on Otter Creek, Ferrisburg, Vermont

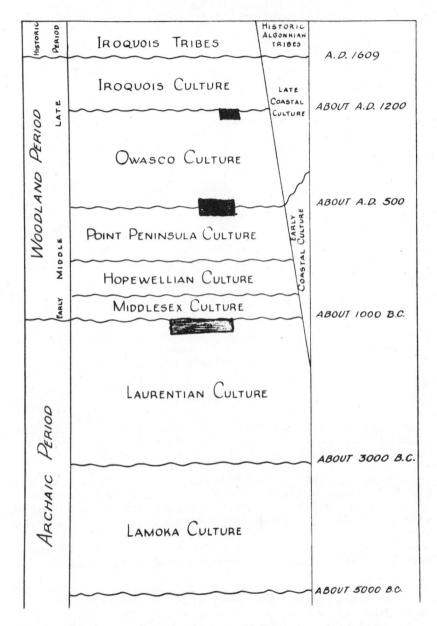

Fig. 1. Cultural Sequence in New York
(Modified and Simplified from Ritchie, 1944)

HISTORIC PERIOD		IROQUOIS TRIBES	HISTORIC ALGONKIAN TRIBES	A.D. 1609
WOODLAND PERIOD	LATE	IROQUOIS CULTURE	LATE COASTAL CULTURE	ABOUT A.D. 1200
		OWASCO CULTURE		ABOUT A.D. 500
	MIDDLE	POINT PENINSULA CULTURE	EARLY COASTAL CULTURE	
		HOPEWELLIAN CULTURE		
	EARLY	MIDDLESEX CULTURE		ABOUT 1000 B.C.
ARCHAIC PERIOD		LAURENTIAN CULTURE		ABOUT 3000 B.C.
		LAMOKA CULTURE		ABOUT 5000 B.C.

Plate No. 5   Blocked areas indicate culture representation
found on Rivers Site. The Culture Sequence in
New York, Ritchie, 1950 Fig. 1

As the work progressed a mantle of black loamy dirt was exposed which rested on undulating surfaces of white mottled clay and yellow sand. In this mantle, at depths varying from 6 - 8 inches from the surface of the ground, many widely scattered, fire-cracked stones were found. It was thought at first that they might have formed a hearth which was subsequently disturbed by plowing, but there were no evidences, such as ash or charcoal, of any hearth; nor was there any indications of plowing, which we understood was extensively done in former years.

Stone chips of chert and quartzite, of various sizes, far outnumbered other material recovered. Finished and broken chipped stone implements, others in the process of manufacture, as well as pottery rim and body sherds, were as widely scattered as were the fire-cracked stones.

Along the eastern shore of Dead River a growth of trees, extending north and south, fringes the point of land. For a distance of eighty feet and westerly from the explorations on the higher land, the trees have been cut down and only their rotting stumps remain.

In this area the land slopes sharply, covering a distance of 25 feet to low water mark. Extending a line horizontally westward, from high water mark to a point directly over low water level, the perpendicular drop is 5 1/2 feet.

On the surface stone chips of chert and quartzite of various sizes were much in evidence and several arrowpoints and weather-beaten sherds of pottery were recovered.

Near the end of the season it was decided to investigate the spot and two areas were chosen for the work.

One was at the southern boundary of the open space where five squares were staked off, comprising 100 square feet. Work proceeded westerly down the slope towards low water mark.

At first a mantle of white sand, an inch in depth, was encountered that covered a clay subsoil. As excavations went deeper in the ground a mixture of black loamy soil and sand, brown in color, was found which continued in depth to two feet at low water level. There were indications that this mixed soil condition extended deeper but water seeped in faster than it could be removed and further work there was stopped.

Many chipped stone implements and sherds of pottery were found. Careful measurements were made of the position of each artifact, but not too much importance was placed on their positions because it was evident that the periodic fluctuations of water levels over the years had caused soil wash, so that the artifacts recovered were probably not in the position in which they were originally deposited.

The next area explored was 30 feet to the north. Using high water level again as the line of demarcation, two squares were excavated westerly and one easterly of it. Here black loamy topsoil was encountered to a depth of 8 inches, resting on a mottled clay subsoil. Soil wash was again in evidence, but not to the extent found in the other area.

As the water level of Dead River receded further, two test pits were dug in a marsh that appeared. They were spaced 2 feet apart, were thirty feet west of low water mark, and 20 inches deep. The soil encountered was a mixture of sand and clay and from each pit numerous broken stone implements and pot sherds were recovered.

PITS

Five pits were uncovered. They were cylindrical in shape and in every instance penetrated into the clay subsoil. They had gently sloping sides and rounded bottoms. There was no evidence that they extended upward into the black loamy top mantle.

They contained small stone chips and crumbs of charcoal and pottery. No artifacts were found in them. The skeletal remains of some fresh water fish, so small and broken that they could not be identified as to species, were found in them.

Bailey found much the same conditions on the John Donovan site situated across Dead River, and raises the question whether they were actually dug pits or depressions caused by rotted tree stumps or erosion that had subsequently become filled with debris.[3]

POST MOLDS

Seventeen post molds were found. With the exception of three, two of which were 3 inches in diameter, the other 3 1/2; they were uniform, with diameters of 4 inches. Their depth in the clay subsoil ranged from 6 - 12 inches. None was found in the yellow sand subsoil, nor did their position indicate the shape of dwelling used by these people.

Rivers Site
Vergennes, Vt.

(Burial No. 1   The outer edge of stones mark perimeter
of the grave. The skull was under cluster
of stones at left.)

Plate No. 6   Burial partially excavated

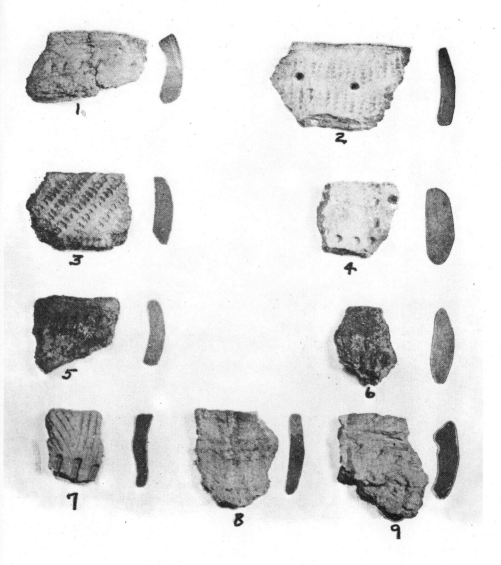

Plate No. 7   Pottery Rim Sherds

1, 9,   Wickham Corded Punctate type

2, 4,   Resembles Wickham Punctate

3,   Jack's Reef Corded

5,   Jack's Reef Corded Punctate

6, 8,   Point Peninsula Corded

7,   Not Typed

Plate No. 8   Pottery Rim Sherds

1,   Resembles Wickham Punctate

2, 4, 5,   Jack's Reef Corded Collar

8,   Wickham Corded Punctate

3,   Jack's Reef Corded

6,   Point Peninsula Plain

7,   Resembles Castle Creek Incised Neck

Plate No. 9   Pottery Body Sherds

1, 3,   Probably Point Peninsula

2,   Light combed body sherd (?)

4,   Coarse Combed body sherd

FIREPLACES

One fireplace was found. It was 30 inches in diameter,
12 inches below the surface of the ground, and 4 inches deep
in the clay subsoil. Its contents consisted of a few scattered
fire-cracked stones, small stone chips, bone fragments, crumbs
of charcoal and pottery sherds. A thin deposit of grey ash was
in evidence around the rim.

BURIALS

One flexed skeleton of an adult male Indian was found,
whose estimated age at the time of death was sixty years.
Clusters of fire-cracked stones marked the perimeter of the
grave (Plate 6.) whose top was 8 inches below the surface of
the ground.

The body had been placed on the right side, head to the
north, and facing west.

The bones were in a bad state of preservation and the
absence of many of them may have been due to disintegration
from long interment in the ground.

Several pottery sherds, broken points of chert and quartzite, granules of charcoal, and the lower jaw of a small rodent
were found scattered about in the grave. A broken bone awl,
made from a deer antler, was near the spine. It was not considered as a grave offering, but had probably been included in
the fill.

BONE

Apart from the broken bone awl, mentioned above, no artifacts made of this material, such as harpoons, spearheads or
fish hooks were found. Two lower jaws of a small rodent, one
a beaver, and the claw core of a bear were the only skeletal
remains of animals found.

PITS

Square No.	Pit No.	Diameter	Depth in Subsoil	Contents
48	1	24"	5"	Black soil, a few fire broken stones and fragments of bone.
96	None			
144	None			
240	None			
335	None			
336	None			
383	2	48"	8"	Stone chips of quartzite and chert, fragments of bone and crumbs of charcoal
384	None			
432	None			
480-528	3	48"	10"	Black soil, stone chips, crumbs of charcoal and bones of fresh water fish that were too small for identification
528-576	4	36"	17"	Black soil, stone chips, small pot sherds and charcoal
528^A-528^B and 576^A	5	36"	32"	Black soil, fire broken stones, fragments of bone, charcoal pottery and rotted wood.

Plate 16

Plate No. 10   Pottery sherds
  1, 2,   Probably Point Peninsula
  3,   Course fabric impressed body sherd
  4, 7,   Corded body sherd
  5, 6,   Pot bases
  8,   Smooth body sherd
  9,   Wickham Corded Punctate

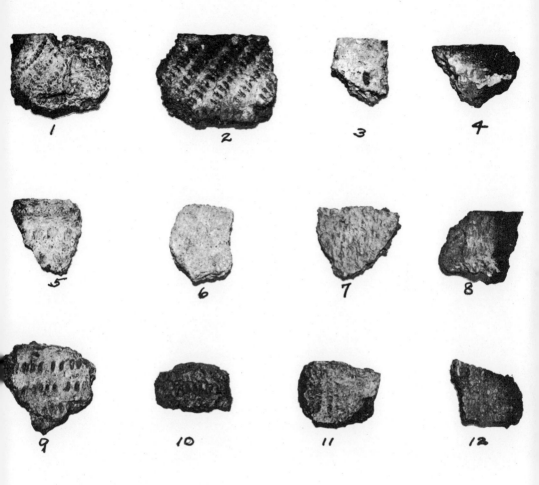

Rivers Site
Vergennes, Vt.

Plate No. 11   Pottery sherds
    1, 2, 3,   Jack's Reef, Corded Collar
    4,   Wickham Corded Punctate
    5, 6, 7, 8,   Point Peninsula Corded
    9, 10, 11, 12,   Probably Point Peninsula - Neck and body sherds

Plate No. 12   Pottery Vessel (Point Peninsula ?)

Courtesy Museum of the American Indian,

Heye Foundation N.Y.

Found at Rivers Site in 1946

POST MOLDS - Their Location and Measurements

Square Number	Post Mold Numbers	Diameter	Depth in Subsoil	Remarks
480	1	4"	12"	
	2	3 1/2"	7"	
	3	4"	7"	
528	1	4"	12"	
	2	4"	11"	
	3	4"	11"	
	4	4"	6"	
	5	4"	10"	
	6	4"	8"	contained rotted wood
	7	4"	8"	
528A	1	3"	8"	" "
	2	4"	12"	
	3	4"	10"	
528B	1	4"	8"	
	2	4"	9"	
576	1	3"	8"	
	2	4"	8"	

Plate 16

CHIPPED STONE IMPLEMENTS

This group comprises a small number of long, broad-bladed, stemmed or side notched spear and arrowpoints (Plate 13, Nos., 26, 30, 31; Plate 14, Nos., 9, 13) of the Laurentian culture.

The majority of the arrowpoints are triangular with straight or concave bases. They range in length from 1 to 2 inches and are evenly divided between chert and quartzite. The chert specimens show a slightly better grade of workmanship than the quartzite, which is probably due to the type of material used.

Two scrapers were recovered, one of mottled chert the other of quartzite. The former is flat on one side, slightly convex on the other, and appears to have been reworked from a rejected implement. One one surface the quartzite scraper shows depressions from which small flakes may have been removed while the other surface is flat and beveled to the scraping edge. Its width is 1 1/2 inches and the one of chert is 1 3/8 inches wide.

Four drills were found, two of mottled chert and two of black chert.

POTTERY

Pottery sherds were recovered from all squares at various depths in the black loamy topsoil, while a few were taken from the yellow sand subsoil, the lowest at a depth of 21 inches below the surface of the ground. Attempts to join sherds together into pot sections have been without success.

Among the more than 300 pottery fragments found the majority are body sherds. Many of them have plain surfaces, while others show parallel lines that may have been drawn with a toothed stick or "comb." (Plates 9 and 10, Nos., 2, 4) Corded or fabric marked surfaces also occur.

The rim interiors are often smoke blackened and on many of them layers of carbonized grease occur. The decorative motif in many cases consists of parallel rows of round depressions while others have no decoration. Rim thicknesses vary from 3/16 to 1/2 inch. Colors range from different shades of brown to muddy yellow. Pottery tempering consists of medium to coarse grit.

CONCLUSIONS

There was not a sufficient number of artifacts recovered nor a large enough area explored to give a complete statistical picture of the cultures occuring on the site.

The recovery of large and heavy, broad-bladed, chipped stone projectile points of the Laurentian culture indicates an early occupation of the area.

The next manifestation recorded is the pottery and triangular arrowheads of the middle and late Woodland period.

It is therefore evident that this area was occupied by two different groups of people, the Laurentians of the older Archaic Period who had no knowledge of agriculture or the use of pottery; followed later by the Woodland peoples with their more complex pottery culture, specialized burial forms and an agricultural economy of corn and beans.[4]

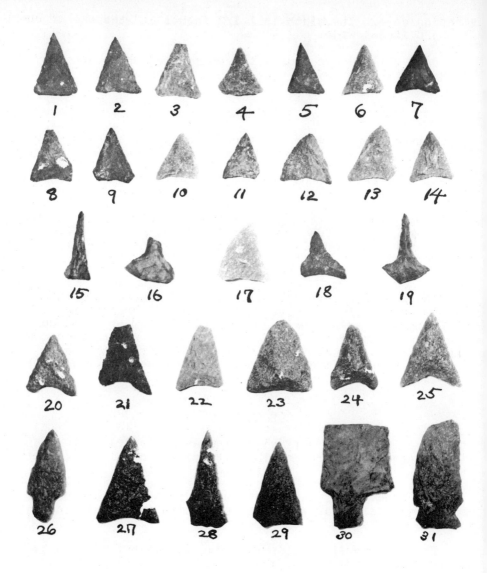

Plate No. 13   Chipped Stone Implements

  1 - 6, 17,   Arrow points, straight base

  7 - 14, 23, 27, 29,   Arrow points, slightly concave base

  15, 16, 18, 19,   Drills

  20, 21, 22, 24, 25,   Arrow points, deep concave base

  26,   Arrow point, broad blade, broad stem (Donovan horizon, Laurentian)

  28,   Arrow point, thin, straight base

  30,   Arrow point, broad blade, broad base (Donovan horizon, Laurentian)

  31,   Knife, side notched, straight base (Donovan horizon, Laurentian)

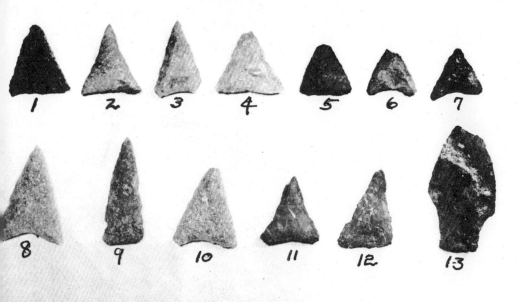

Plate No. 14   Chipped Stone Implements

1, 2, 4, 5, 12,   Arrow points, straight base

3, 6, 10, 11, 7,   Arrow points, slight concave base

8,   Arrow point, deep concave base

9,   Thin, side notched Arrow point

13,   Broad bladed, broad stemmed Arrow point
                     (Donovan Horizon, Laurentian)

14, 15,   End scrapers

Plate No. 15 Bone implements from Rivers Site on Otter Creek

But there appears to have been a span of nearly 1500
years between these occupations with no recorded evidence of
the early Woodland period, as seen in New York.   It cannot be
assumed that the absence of manifestations of that period
would indicate that the area was unpopulated during that
space of time, as further excavations might produce the miss-
ing evidence; which if found would be a significant contri-
bution not only to Vermont archeology but to the prehistory
of the northeast in general.

NOTES

1. Bailey, 1939, p. 104
2. Ritchie, 1944, p. 7;
            1950, Fig. 1;
            1951, p. 132
3. Bailey, 1939 a, p. 6
4. Ritchie, 1950, pp. 4-9

* *

<u>Indian Artifact Displays</u>

    More or less adequate collections of Indian Artifacts are
on display at the Sheldon Museum, Middlebury, Vt.; Fairbanks
Museum, St. Johnsbury, Vt.; Windham County Museum, Newfane, Vt.;
Bennington Museum, Bennington, Vt.   Mr. Morris Crandall of
Springfield, Vermont has a very fine private collection.

Our Indian Archeology Exhibit

by Horace Eldred,
Director, Robert Hull Fleming Museum
The University of Vermont
January, 1942

It is usual to class Archeology specimens as objects not definitely associated with an historic tribe. This grouping is justifiable for, in the main, these objects belong to an earlier time stratum than those that can be definitely assigned to living peoples. The specimens in the Fleming Exhibit were probably recovered from the North Atlantic area.

This area includes all of New England and the Maritime Provinces of Canada. Its general archeological characteristics are: extensive shell deposits on the coast; pottery, crude with rudely stamped decorations; bone occasionally used for implements and ornaments; extensive steatite quarries and vessels of the same material; and, finally, great numbers of rock shelters.

Plummets are a group of pre-historic pendant-like objects of stone, bone, shell, copper, and other materials, the origin and use of which are numerous and varied. Many specimens are rudely shaped, but the greater number are highly finished and symmetric, and often graceful in contour. Usually there is a shallow encircling groove, as shown by the plummet in the case; occasionally there are two at the upper end; and in rare cases one or more grooves or ridges encircle the body of the longer specimens at different points giving a spindle-like effect. The original plummets may have been net sinkers, or other objects having at first only practical functions, which in time came to be regarded as luck stones or charms, passing gradually into general use as such, with many shades of significance and widely divergent forms. The stone plummet shown in the case was probably used by the Indians of North America as a line sinker or net sinker, its use being entirely practical owing to its crude shape and form.

Sinew Stones are usually rudely shaped as shown by the specimen in the case. They may be natural pebbles, boulders, or fragments but by prolonged use they have assumed definite shapes or have been intentionally modified to better fit them for their purpose. They were used for stretching and drying the sinew used by the Indian tribes as thread for sewing purposes. Sinew stones varied in size according to the thickness of the fiber twisted around them.

Pottery. It seems that the art of pottery making was not indigenous to the North Atlantic States. It consisted mainly of simple culinary utensils, mostly rounded on conical bodies bowls and pots decorated with angular incised lines and textile imprintings. The fragment of pottery shown in the case is a typical example of this type of pottery. Similar fragments of pottery have been found in shell heaps and burial grounds throughout the North Atlantic area.

Banner Stones. A name applied to a group of pre-historic objects of polished stone, which for lack of definite information as to their use, are assigned to the problematical class. Their form is exceedingly varied, but certain funda-mental features of their shape are practically unvarying, and are of such a nature as to suggest the use of the term "banner stones". These features are the axial perforations and the extension of the body or mid rib into two wing-like projections Of the various forms the most typical is that which suggests a two bladed ax, as illustrated by the banner stone in the case. Nothing is definitely known of the particular significance attached to these objects, or of the manner of their use, save by inference from their form and the known customs of the tribes. It appears probably, from the presence of perforations, that they were mounted for use on a staff, on a handle as a ceremonial weapon, or on the stem of a calumet. The perfora-tion is cylindrical, and is bored with great precision longi-tudinally through the thick portion of the mid rib. Banner stones are found in burial mounds and on formerly inhabited sites in all parts of New England.

Arrow Points and Spear Heads. The shape of the stone arrow point is usually triangular or pointed oval, though some of them have very slender blades with expanding base. Many of them are notched. In stone implements of this class the only line of distinction between arrow points and spear heads is that of size. Very few stone arrow points are as much as two inches long, and these are quite slender; thick or strong ones are much shorter. Solid flesh, being almost as resistant as soft rubber, could not be penetrated by a large projectile unless it were propelled from a bow without arificial aid which is not at the command of a savage. The arrow points and the spear head shown in the case are typical eastern forms. They were probably recovered from a burial mound or shell heap in one of the New England States.

Bone Beads, were usually cylinders produced by cutting sections of various lengths from the thigh or other parts of the vertebrate skeletons. When the wall of the bone was thick the ends were ground to give a spherical form. The general uses to which beads were put are legion. They were tied in the hair, worn singly or in strings from the ears, on the neck, arms, wrist, waist, and lower limbs, or were attached to bark and wooden vessels, matting, basketry and other textiles. They were largely employed as gifts and as money, also as tokens and in records of hunts or of important events such as treaties. They were regarded as insignia of functions and were often buried in vast quantities with the dead.

Knives. Cutting tools were indispensable to primitive men, and the greatest ingenuity was exercised in their manufacture. These objects were shaped by chipping or flaking processes. They were largely leaf-shaped, as shown by the stone knives in the case. In shaping the blades, a suitable piece of brittle stone was selected, and with a hammerstone, chips were removed by means of vigorous blows about the periphery, alternating the faces. The larger blades, some of which are upward of 2 feet in length, require skill of a high order for their successful elaboration. In making small implements, such as those in the case, from fragments of proximate form, the hammer is not required, the work being accomplished with a piece of stone or hard bone. The uses of these knives were innumerable; they served in war and were indispensable in every branch of the arts of life. They also served in symbolism and ceremony.

Celts are ungrooved axes or hatchets of stone, metal or other hard material. It is uncertain whether the name is derived from the Latin celtis, "chisel", to which the instrument bears some resemblance, or from the Welsh cellt, a "flint stone". The celts range in weight from less than half an ounce to more than twenty pounds, while the diversity of form is very great. Their distribution is more general than that of the grooved ax. The primary purpose was probably that of a hatchet, but in one shape or another they served as adzes, chisels, scrapers, skinning knives, meat cutters and weapons. Celts made of brittle stone, similar to the specimen shown in the case, were shaped mainly by flaking. In most, the edge was more or less sharpened by grinding and sometimes the entire implement was partially smoothed in the same way. Many have the surface roughened by pecking at the top, which was inserted in a cavity cut in a wooden club; in others, this roughening was around the middle, to give a firmer grip to a withe handle. Numerous celts are found where hard brittle stone is abundant in the New England States.

Gouges are stone implements resembling celts or adzes with one face hollowed out, giving a curbed edge. Early writers speak of their use as spouts, in some sections, for tapping maple sugar trees, the sap running through the groove into the vessel placed beneath. Examples grooved for hafting are rate. The gouge and celt are often indistinguishable. This close resemblance is illustrated by the specimens in the case.

Bone Awls were universal among Indians from the earliest times, and are one of the familiar archeologic objects recovered from excavations in pre-historic sites. Perhaps most Indians preferred deer bone as a material for awls, but bear and turkey bones and deer antler were also extensively employed. The fibula of the deer merely needed sharpening to produce the tool. The awl was used to make perforations through which thread of sinew or other sewing material was passed, when skins for moccasins, clothing, tents, etc. were sewed, and in quill work, bead work, and basket work. Other uses for awls were for making holes for pegs in woodwork, as a gauge in canoe making, for shredding sinew, for graving, etc. Rude awls similar to the one in the case, formed by grinding to a point a long bone or sliver of a bone, are frequently encountered in graves and on the sites of early habitations in the North Atlantic area.

Drills. The first drill, similar to the specimen shown in the case, was a development of a primitive awl. It was a sharp pointed instrument of stone which was held in one hand, pressed against the object, and turned back and forth until a hole was bored. The point was usually set in a socket of bone or wood. By setting it in a transverse handle, increased pressure and leverage were obtained, with increased penetrating power. Artificially perforated objects of bone, fish bones, ivory, pottery, stone, and wood, common to all periods in the world's history, are found in caves, shell heaps, and burial places of the Indians. The holes vary from an eighth to a half inch in diameter, and from a fourth of an inch to six inches or more in depth. The point used is indicated by the form of the perforation. This simple form of drill is found in large numbers on burial grounds and on formerly inhabited sites in all parts of the North Atlantic area.

Hoes. Certain stone implements have been found in vast numbers which are generally conceded to have been used in breaking the soil. Of these the most characteristic are the hoes. The most common form has an oval, or elliptical outline with ends either rounded or somewhat pointed similar to the hoe shown in the case. The larger implements of this class are generally dominated spades, and the shorter forms hoes; but as both had the handles put on either parallel with the longer axis or at an angle with it, allowing all alike to be used in the same manner, the distinction is without particular significance.

Axes. The grooved ax takes a prominent place among the stone implements used by the northern tribes. The normal form, similar to the one in the case, is that of a thick wedge, with rounded angles and an encircling groove near the top for securing the handle, but there is a great variation

from the average. Usually the instrument was made of some
hard tough stone, but where this was not available softer
material was utilized, when not made from boulders closely
approximating in shape the desired implement, the ax was
roughed by chipping and was reduced to the desired shape by
pecking with a hard stone and by grinding. It is probable
that the ax served various purposes in the arts, and especially in war and in the chase. The grooved ax is said to
have been used in felling trees and in cutting them up, but
it is manifestly not well suited for such work. Numerous
specimens are found in the steatite or soap stone quarries of
New England and the Maritime Provinces of Canada, where they
were used for cutting out masses of this rock.

Pitted Hammer Stones are employed in shaping stones,
especially in the more advanced stages of the work. They are
unhafted and are held tightly in the hand for delivering heavy
blows, or lightly between the thumb and finger tips for flaking
or pecking. They may be natural pebbles, boulders, or fragments, but by prolonged use they assume definite shapes or are
intentionally modified to better fit them for their purpose.
Globular forms, similar to the hammer stone in the case, pre-
vail and the variety employed in pecking and for other light
uses often has shallow depressions centrally placed at opposite
sides to render the finger hold more secure.

NOTE   For many years the Fleming Indian Archaeology Exhibit
     was loaned to Vermont schools. Since 1950 this service
     has been discontinued; THE EXHIBIT SHOULD BE RESTORED AND
     CIRCULATED.

INDIANS IN EASTERN VERMONT

Excerpts from Pages 585-592
History of Eastern Vermont
By Benjamin H. Hall
New York: D. Appleton   Co. 1858

Of the aboriginal inhabitants of that part of Vermont
which borders the banks of the Connecticut, very little is
known. The Iroquois Indians, whose hunting-ground comprehended
the whole of the western portion of the state, seldom extended
their wanderings across the mountains, and have left but few
vestiges of their presence, even in the places which were most
frequented by them. The country in the neighborhood of Lunen-
burgh and Newbury, and on the side of the river opposite to
the latter place, was called by the Indians, "Coos," which word,
in the Abenaqui language, is said to signify "The Pines." At
these localities, and at other points on the upper Connecticut,
formerly resided a branch of the Abenaqui tribe. On the 8th
of May, 1725, occurred a memorable fight at the lower village
of Pigwacket, New Hampshire, which resulted in the defeat,
by Capt. John Lovewell and thirty-four men, of a large Indian
force, commanded by the chiefs Paugus and Wahwa. After this
event the "Coosucks," as the Indians were called who inhabited
the Coos country, deserted their abodes, and removing to Canada
became identified there with the tribe at S. Francis. Subsequent to the reduction of Canada by the English, in 1760,
several Indian families returned to Coos, and remained there
until they became extinct.

The extent of the Indian settlements at Newbury has never
been fully ascertained. The character of the country was such
as would naturally suit the taste of those who depended upon
hunting and fishing for support, for the woods were filled with
bears, moose, deer, and game, while the Connecticut abounded
in salmon, and the brooks were alive with trout. Of the evidences of savage life which have been found in this vicinity,
the following account by a citizen of Newbury may be relied on
as correct. "On the high ground, east of the mouth of Cow
Meadow brook, and south of the three large projecting rocks,
were found many indications of an old and extensive Indian
settlement. There were many domestic implements. Among the
rest were a stone mortar and pestle. The pestle I have seen.
Heads of arrows, large quantities of ashes, and the ground
burnt over to a great extent, are some of the marks of a long
residence there. The burnt ground and ashes were still visible
the last time the place was ploughed. On the meadow, forty or
fifty rods below, near the rocks in the river, was evidently
a burying-ground. The remains of many of the sons of the
forest are there deposited. Bones have frequently been turned
up by the plough. That they were buried in the sitting
posture, peculiar to the Indians, has been ascertained. When
the first settlers came here, the remains of a fort were still
visible on the Ox Bow, a dozen or twenty rods from the east
end of Moses Johnson's lower garden, on the south side of the

lane. The size of the fort was plain to be seen. Trees about as large as a man's thigh, were growing in the circumference of the fort. A profusion of white flint-stones and heads of arrows may yet be seen scattered over the ground."

The picture writing of the Indians, which is to be seen in two localities in Eastern Vermont, affords satisfactory evidence of the fact, that certain tribes were accustomed to frequent the Connecticut and the streams connected with it, even though they were not actual residents of the pleasant banks within which those waters are confined. At the foot of Bellows Falls, and on the west side of the channel of the Connecticut, are situated two rocks, on which are inscribed figures, the meaning of which it is difficult to determine. The larger rock presents a group of variously ornamented heads. The surface which these heads occupy is about six feet in height and fifteen feet in breadth. Prominent among the rest is the figure occupying nearly a central position in the group. From its head, which is supported by a neck and shoulders, six rays or feathers extend, which may be regarded as emblems of excellence or power. Four of the other heads are adorned each with a pair of similar projections. On a separate rock, situated a short distance from the main group, a single head is sculptured, which is finished with rays or feathers, and was probably intended to designate an Indian chief. The length of the head, exclusive of the rays, is fourteen inches, and its breadth across the forehead in its widest part is ten inches. These sculpturings seem to have been intended to commemorate some event in which a chief and a number of his tribe performed some noted exploit, or met with some sad disaster. The former supposition is undoubtedly the more correct. It is well known that the Indians were usually careful to conceal the traces of their misfortunes, and eager to publish the evidence of their successes.

The rocks are situated about eight rods south of the bridge for common travel, across the Falls. That on which the group is pictured is, during much of the time, under water. The other, which is further from the river, is not so much affected by the wash of the stream. Whenever a freshet occurs, both are covered. An idea of the locality of these sculpturings may be obtained from the accompanying engraving. The view presented is from a point between the two noted rocks, which are respectively designated by the letters A and B. A train on the Sullivan Railroad is seen passing up on the other side of the river. In the background rise the mountains of New Hampshire.

On the south bank of the Wantastiquet or West river, in the town of Brattleborough, is situated the "Indian Rock." Its location is about one hundred rods west of the point of junction of the Wantastiquet and Connecticut rivers. It lies low, and during a part of the year is covered with water, or with sand and dirt, the deposit of the river. On first examining this rock, the figures on the upper part of it were alone visible. Just below them, the rock was covered with

Indian Sculptures

History of Eastern Vermont
Benjamin H. Hall
p. 587

Portion of inscriptions on Indian Rock south side of West River, near Brattleboro, Vermont, now under water due to the building of a dam in the Connecticut River.

Drawn from a photograph taken in 1866. (Antiquities of New England Indians, Charles C. Willoughby, page 169)

The Colchester Jar
One of the best specimens
of Iroquoian pottery ever
unearthed. On view at
Robert Hull Fleming Museum,
University of Vermont,
Burlington

Indian Sculptures
at Bellows Falls
as they appeared
in 1958. Compare
with drawings from
Hall's History of
Eastern Vermont.

earth to the depth of six inches. The earth was removed,
until a surface measuring ten feet in width, and eight feet
in height, was exposed. At the point where the workmen ceased
digging, the rock was covered with three feet of earth. The
whole surface of the rock, was, upon closer scrutiny, found to
be covered with inscriptions. Among these the date 1755 was
to be distinguished. The two figures in the upper corner of
the engraving, and on a line with one another, are each about
eight inches in height, and six inches across, measuring from
the extremities of the lateral appendages. Of the ten figures
here presented, six are supposed to designate birds, two bear
a resemblance to snakes, one is not unlike a dog or a wolf,
and one conveys no idea either of bird, beast, or reptile.
The chiselling of these sculptures is deeper and more easily
traced than that of the sculptures at Bellows Falls. Icono-
graphic skill may detect the meaning of these configurations.
The impression, which one unused to the study of hieroglyphics
receives from an examination of them, is that they are the
work of the Indians, and that they were carved by them merely
for amusement, while watching at this spot for game, or while
resting after the toils of the chase.

    Such are the most important memorials of the Indians
which are to be found in Eastern Vermont. Regarded as specimens of the rude and uncultivated attempts of a now decaying
race to express their ideas, however unimportant those ideas
may have been, they cannot but be viewed with mingled emotions
of curiosity and respect.

INDIANS GROUPS IN VERMONT

By John C. Huden

I. The Pre-Algonkians, ?? B.C. - 2000 B.C. ??

    Unmistakable evidences of Pre-Algonkian (and Eskimo?) cultures have been found all over New England and New York.

    Pre-Algonkian sinkers and fish-lures have been unearthed in Hubbardton; polished slate knives at Swanton; whale-tail ceremonial objects in the Otter Creek region. All these bear witness that Pre-Algonkian people lived and died in Vermont.

    Long before the dawn of history these people were pushed out of New England by the "Old Algonkian" stock.

II. The Old Algonkians, 2000 B.C. - 1300 A.D. ?

    Old Algonkian pottery together with other implements have been discovered in every state east of the Mississippi River and north of the Tennessee-Carolina regions.

    Some of the best artifacts of Old Algonkian origin were discovered at Swanton in the 1870's, and near Orwell 1933-1934.

    It is probable that further archaeological research would reveal many other Old Algonkian and Pre-Algonkian sites in Vermont.

III. Recent Algonkians, 1200 A.D. - 1790 A.D.

    All these tribes or sub-groups spoke Algonkian dialects. They could understand each other fairly well, and as a rule hated the Iroquois. In fact, Iroquois is a an Algonkian word meaning "real adder snakes," not exactly a term of endearment. The ancient hatred between these two great Indian groups arose partly because the Iroquois split the Algonkians in terrible wars which left the Iroquois in possession of central New York and the St. Lawrence estuary.

1. Abnakis (Abenakis, Ouabenaki, Waubanakee, etc.) "Dawn People," "People of the East." Along Lake Champlain from Missisquoi Bay to Otter Creek and possibly to Chimney Point; around Lake Bomoseen; around Lake Memphremagog; along the Connecticut River and tributaries from Canada south to the Ottauquechee, at least.

2. Ammonoosucks
   "Narrow fishing-place people." Wells River, Barnet,
   McIndoe Falls, etc. (Probably Pennacooks?)

3. Arisagunticooks (Alsignotigak, etc.)
   "People who live near the river abounding in shells."
   Along the St. Francis River in Quebec from Lake
   Memphremagog and vicinity northward. Sometimes called
   also Coaticooks, "People at the Pines." Probably sub-
   groups of the Abnaki; possibly mixed with Kenebekis.

4. Coosucks
   "Pine-tree place. People." Newbury, Ryegate, Barnet,
   Bradford, Fairlee, Thetford. Probably Pennacooks.

5. Kenebekis
   "People at the Long Lake." Averill, Canaan, Bloomfield.
   Probably Abnakis from the headwaters of the Kennebec;
   possibly some Pennacooks.

6. Kikomkwaks
   "Those who live near sucker-fishing places."
   Bradford, Newbury, Orleans, etc. Probably Pennacooks.

7. Mahicans (Mohicans) "River-Folk"; "People of the Ebbing
   Tide"; and "Wolf-People." (In the 1600's, Mohicans
   occupied the Hudson Valley east shore. They were
   broken up by English, Dutch and Mohawks, and driven
   north before 1750.) Hoosic Valley, Pownal; West
   Arlington; Back Bay, near Fair Haven; Lake Bomoseen,
   Lake Hortonia, etc.; mouth of Winooski river;
   Missisquoi Bay. Probably also at Squakheag (Vernon,
   Guilford, Brattleboro and Putney.) During King
   Phillip's War, 1675-1676.

8. Mississiak (Missisquatucks; Missisquois, etc.)
   "People at the marshy, grassy place (which abounds in
   in waterfowl?)" Missisquoi Bay, Swanton, Highgate, etc.
   The Mississiak were Abnakis plus Algonkian refugees
   from New York and New England, together with a few
   Hurons from Ancien-Lorette, Quebec. Missisquoi Bay
   and its environs was an outpost of the St. Francis
   (now Odanak) Abnakis.

9. Nulheganocks
   "Trapping-place people" or, "People who use wooden
   deadfall traps." These were probably Abnakis or
   Pennacooks who trapped along the Nulhegan River,
   (Brighton, Ferdinand, Brunswick, Maidstone.)

10. Obom Sawin (Bomaseens, Bomzeens, etc.)
    Probably a band of Abnakis, but possibly Mohicans,
    (or perhaps both) who lived around Lake Hortonia and
    Lake Bomoseen, "Indian Fields" in Castleton.

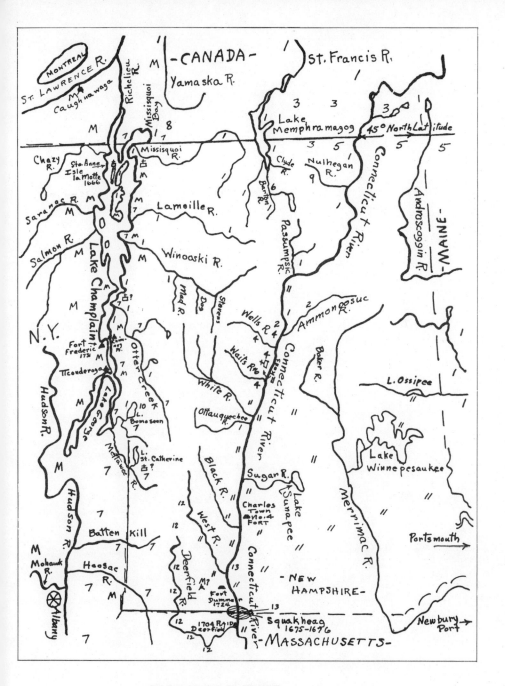

INDIAN GROUPS IN VERMONT

Numbers refer to Algonkian Indian groups; Captial M
shows Mohawk sites. Se article "Indian Groups in Vermont"
for key statements.

11. Pennacooks
   "People of the Foot Hills"; "People at the Bottom of
   High Land." Southern and western New Hampshire, as far
   west as Connecticut River from Bernardston,
   Massachusetts, northward to Newbury or Barnet.
   Pennacook pictographs have been found in Bellows Falls;
   other traces of these peaceful people indicate that
   they also lived in considerable numbers at Vernon,
   Brattleboro, Springfield, Weathersfield, and
   Westminster.

12. Pocumtucks (Pocomtooks, etc.)
   "People of the very narrow swift river." (?) Until the
   destruction of their "fort" (near Deerfield,
   Massachusetts) by the Mohawks in 1666 the Pocumtucks
   were located in western Massachusetts and southwestern
   Vermont, especially the Deerfield valley. Their village
   Squakheag was near Northfield, Massachusetts.

13. Squakheags
   "People Who Catch Fish With Pointed Spears."
   "People of the Broad River Fishing-Place." In 1674-
   1676 these Algonkians included remnants of Massachusetts,
   Connecticut, Rhode Island, New Hampshire and New York
   tribes gathered under Metacomet "King Philip." See
   also Pennacooks and Pocumtucks.

IV. The Iroquoians, 1300 A.D. ?- 1790 A.D., etc.

        The Mohawks in 1550 controlled Eastern New York north
   of the Mohawk river, plus all of Lake Champlain and the
   Richelieu river which on old maps are called respectively
   "The Sea of the Iroquois" and "Iroquois River." It is
   not surprising, therefore, that Mohawk pottery, arrowheads and other evidences are found in western Vermont,
   often mixed with Algonkian goods.

        The Iroquois jar discovered at Colchester, Vermont,
   in 1825 is one of the best of its kind. It is on display
   in the Robert Hull Fleming Museum at the University of
   Vermont, Burlington.

        The Mohawks (probably) had outposts at Alburg,
   Swanton, Milton, Colchester, Monkton, Addison, Shoreham,
   Orwell and near Brattleboro.

        In Massachusetts and Connecticut towns west of the
   Connecticut river, every two years a deputation of Mohawks
   were feared as far east as Castine, Maine, so it is fair
   to assume that they axacted their levies north of the
   Massachusetts line, too.

HISTORY AND CONDITION OF THE STATE CABINET

INDIAN RELICS
1908-1910
by
George H. Perkins, Ph. D.

While the collection of Indian Relics is not as large as
it should be it is yet fairly representative of the different
forms that have been found in the State and contains some very
excellent and finely made specimens. If those who have in their
possession a few of these objects would contribute them to the
State Collection they would be far more useful, because more
accessible to those wishing to study them and a very large numbe
of specimens from the same region are much more instructive
when seen together than they can be if divided into small lots
which are more or less widely separated.

There are undoubtedly many of stone implements scattered
about the State which are for the most part unknown to archeologists and which must continue hidden so long as they are
distributed, a few on one farm and a few on another, but which
would add materially to our knowledge of ancient Vermont if they
could be placed together where they could be readily seen and
studied. For this reason I am tempted to use this opportunity
to urge all who have any such relics to deposit them in the
State Museum, if they are not willing to give them or sell
them. Setting aside the rudest and less perfect specimens, of
which there are a good many, we have some three hundred and
fifty good specimens from Vermont and a few from other states.
These latter are mostly exceptionally good specimens. There
are among them some mining hammers from the copper mines of
Lake Superior, a few perfect pieces of pottery from mounds in
Ohio, polished celts, amulets, etc., from other parts of the
United States.

Of the Vermont specimens, some are quite peculiar to this
region, others are similar to those found in the west.

Those special localities, such as mounds, graves, caches,
village sites, etc., which in other parts of the country have
afforded such large collections of prehistoric objects, are
almost wholly lacking in Vermont as they are in most parts of
the eastern United States. Still there are one or two places
from which many and very interesting objects have been taken.

The most notable of these is an ancient burial ground
not far north of the railroad station at East Swanton. As a
considerable number of the most valuable objects obtained at
this place are now in the State Collection, a somewhat detailed account of it will not be out of place here.

In the _Proceedings of the American Association for the
Advancement of Science, Volume XXII_, the writer published the

first account of this very interesting site. This article was
accompanied by several plates illustrating the specimens found
and those who may care to see a more full account than can be
given here are referred to it. The main facts, however, are
given here.

The locality is a sand ridge, which appears to have been
covered by a forest of Norway pines. About fifty years ago,
after a portion of the trees had been cut off, and the sand
blown away in places, it was discovered that the ground on
which the trees had been growing was once used as a burial
ground, for a number of graves were found and examined. If,
as was stated by some of those who found implements there,
some of them were taken from beneath large stumps, it must
have been long since the graves were made, for it must have
been before the forest had begun to grow.

At the time when Europeans came into the region, the
Indian occupants were Algonkins and a tribe of these, the St.
Francis, had a village four or five miles down the Missisquoi,
which they occupied until comparatively recent times, that is,
until the Revolution.
It is said that these St. Francis Indians had no knowledge
of the ancient burial ground and if we may judge from the
objects found, the people who used it were not Algonkins, or
at least not like those who came later.

These had a burial ground farther down the river, which
I have examined. In the old cemetery which, as has been stated,
was not suspected until the wind had driven off a part of the
sand and disclosed some of the graves, or at least some of the
implements, thus leading to the discovery of the graves. At
least twenty-five graves have been found. Those first opened
by Mr. Elliot Frink, from whom most of the Montpelier specimens
came, were six feet below the surface, but some of those since
investigated were not more than two feet from the top of the
ground because of the removal of the surface sand by the wind.

The sand in which the graves were dug is of a light brown
color, but in some cases, perhaps all except two, the sand
immediately about the bodies was stained a deep red brown.
There were two graves, however, in which the sand at the bottom
was black. The finding in one of the graves of a piece of red
hematite, which is in the case at Montpelier, explains the red
color. Apparently, the sand was colored, perhaps as a part of
the funeral rites, by pouring over it a mixture of hematite and
water. This appears the more likely since many of the stone
objects found in the graves are stained so that, apparently,
the grave had received the body and such objects as were to be
buried with it before the coloring fluid was poured over the
whole.

Most of the bones found in these graves were badly decayed.
So far as I know, only a femur, a radius and about half of a
skull are all that were rescued. These were stained green in

parts by copper carbonate, which came from the copper implements found with them.

The portion of a skull from one of these graves is quite
perfect, tho the bones are much discolored and as has been
stated stained greenish by copper carbonite. Nearly all of
the right half is preserved. It is of a medium sized adult.
No teeth remain and only five alveoli. The condyles and
foramen are entire.

None of those who examined these graves can give much
information as to the position of the skeletons in the graves,
whether horizontal or, as was not uncommon among the aborigines,
in a sitting posture, but from such facts as it has been possible to obtain it seems probable that the latter was the case.

Mr. Frink stated that he opened one grave in which the
skeleton was in a vertical position, head down, and that in
this grave nothing except a few arrow heads was found. If
this body was buried in this position it is a very unusual case.
It seems more likely that the body was buried sitting and had
at some time, either during the excavation or before, fallen
over and the skull, dropping down between the feet, would seem
to have been placed originally below the rest of the body.

In all I have seen about a hundred specimens that were
taken from these graves. The graves were all excavated before
I came into the State and therefore only hearsay evidence concerning them is available. Fortunately, there were in Swanton
several persons, who were intelligently interested in such
things, and I have no reason to doubt the essential correct-
ness of their statements.

As to the objects found in the graves, mention will be
made of them later. In general, it may here be noticed that a
few copper implements and ornaments, a number of shell beads,
stone tubes, celts, amulets, bird-head stones, two-hole stones,
boat-stones, discoidal stone, numerous arrow and spear points
were taken from the graves. Also several nondescript articles.
One of these is a gnarled mass of spruce about as large as
one's two fists.

It has a spheroidal form and bears upon its surface several
rounded, conical protuberances. Several objects which would
not ordinarily attract attention were also found, such as a
smooth white quartz pebble and two pieces of fossiliferous
stone, has they not been found in graves.

Figures 25-7 pl. H, 101, I, 3,5,7 Pl. K. show some of the
Swanton specimens in the State Collection. Others are shown
on other places.

As illustrating, tho less completely than might be desired,
the archeology of Vermont, the specimens at Montpelier deserve
a somewhat detailed notice. Accordingly, the different classes

- 46 -

of objects will be taken up and briefly described with such illustrations as it has been found possible to give. Such an account as that which follows is the more important because, as is well known, these relics of aboriginal occupation are seldom found at present and most of those now in collections can never be duplicated.

Beginning with those objects that are everywhere most abundant we first consider the

Chipped and Flaked Implements.

There are certain common forms of chipped or flaked stone implements, which have been fashioned in much the same way all over the world. In making his first and necessarily rude implements, man, wherever he lived, appears to have worked in substantially the same manner and therefore to have produced very nearly the same results. It is a fact, very easily verified by anyone who will take the trouble to examine these ruder and simpler implements in any large museum, that such objects are very similar, whether from northern Asia, southern Africa, Europe or America. There is a certain amount of difference due to difference in the material used and usually, while there is general resemblance, there are a few pieces found in each locality, which are unlike those from any other place. Naturally, the most commonly used material is that most easily obtained in the locality occupied by the makers. The most accessible stone which can be used is always the source of most of the specimens in any given locality, but almost always some of the specimens are made from finer and more attractive stone than most localities afford.

The above remarks apply fully to our Vermont collections.

There is a bluish gray quartzite which is found in ledges in different parts of the State and from this by far the larger part of the chipped objects, arrow and spear points, knives, etc., were made. Very many other sorts of stone were also used, tho much less commonly. Agate, jasper, hornstone, milky or crystalline quartz and other materials occur in Vermont in the drift gravels or in seams in ledges of other rock and all these were used now and then, especially when some elegant point was to be fashioned.

Undoubtedly some material was imported, that is traded for, from the west where handsome material suited to this purpose is more common than in New England.

As the most common material used was the gray quartzite, so the most commonly found chipped implements are triangular and without haft or barbs. These triangular objects are of many sizes from those that are scarcely more than half an inch long, to the large spears or knives that may be five or even six inches long. The proportions of the triangle varies also indefinitely. Some are slender, others nearly or quite, as long as wide.

The specimens in the upper row in Plate V, are of this sort. The forms here shown are perhaps the most common in Vermont. While these triangular points may occur made of various sorts of silicious stone, the gray quartzite mentioned above is more frequently used than any other material.

This triangular form appears to have been the ordinary everyday point and few are as delicately finished or as perfectly regular in shape as some of the more elaborate stemmed and barbed points.

As compared with similar points found in the Ohio Valley and elsewhere, our Vermont specimens are usually less finely made and of less attractive material, but those few that are our very best cannot be surpassed by specimens from any locality.

The specimens shown in the second row on Plate V are many of them from the Swanton graves mentioned above. Probably these were mostly used as knives and they differ somewhat from other specimens found in the State, as they are thinner and of different material.

They are made of a dark gray or bluish hornstone, which chips very smoothly, leaving a fine, even surface.

The specimens shown at the bottom of Plate V represent very well some of the less common tho not very infrequently found Vermont specimens.

The four specimens forming a diagonal series beginning with the lower right hand corner, are somewhat puzzling, for, while they and others similar are almost always exceedingly well shaped and finished, they are made of slate, red, purple or gray, a material not hard enough to withstand much usage nor are they strong enough to bear much strain.

Nevertheless, they occur, tho somewhat rarely, in sufficient numbers to convince one that they had a definite and important place in the economy of the aborigines. They are nearly always stemmed and more or less completely barbed as the figures show. Naturally, made from such material, they were never chipped, but ground, and the surface is usually very nicely smoothed. They were probably knives, to be used perhaps in dressing skins or such other work as did not require hard usage.

In the University Museum at Burlington there is one of these slate knives which is eight and three quarters inches long and only an inch and a half wide at the largest part. Such an implement, if such it was, could not have endured any usage except the most careful.

All the figures on Plate V are somewhat less than half natural size. The largest slate point for example is nearly six inches long.

PLATE V.

Vermont Stone Implements—Arrow and Spear Points, Knives.
One-half actual size.

PLATE VI.

Vermont Stone Implements—Knives and Spear Points.
One-half actual size.

All there are of the figures should be reckoned in the same way, that is, enlarged to a little more than twice the size on the plate.

Plate VI shows a few of the largest of our chipped specimens. All the figures are shown on the plate somewhat less than half full size. Those in the top row may have been intended to be used as either spears or knives. The longest is seven and a half inches in length and, as the figure shows, it is is quite slender and very well made. The large leaf-shaped object is well made, tho not finely finished. It is eight and a half inches long and may have been used in dressing skins or it may have been a hoe or spade as it closely resembles western implements. The lowest figure on Plate VI is another of the largest chipped implements that have been found. It is of the common gray quartzite and is ten inches long and at the widest part two inches. It is light gray quartz and very well made.

Plate VII shows some of the more common scrapers and drills. The Scrapers are easily recognized by the abruptly bevelled edge. All of the figures in the upper row, down the left side and across the bottom of the plate are of this sort. As is readily seen, the form may vary greatly, but in all the peculiar scraping edge is present.

The drills, too, are usually easily recognizable by the pointed and often polished end. Some of these drills are remarkable specimens of chipped work. The two longest in the center of the Plate VII show how it was possible for skilled workmen to chip from a flinty bit of stone a very slender point. The longest of the drills figured is over four inches from end to end.

The figures on this plate are somewhat more than one half full size.

Most of the chipped objects are of small size, but occasionally larger implements were made in this way. One or two axes and some other sorts of implement were chipped or flaked, usually from rather thin plates of quartzite. Sometimes, tho very rarely, thicker pieces of silicious stone were used as is seen in the celt at the bottom of Plate IX. This, however, is unique in that after the general form had been made by striking off flakes of the hornstone of which it is made, the entire surface was somewhat smoothed by rubbing or grinding and the edge, as the figure shows, was ground very smooth and sharp.

The axes, celts, gouges, etc., were nearly always broken into something like the desired form and then, by what must have been a slow and laborious process, rubbed into shape on another stone with the aid of sand and water. Of course, when a water worn pebble was found which had such form that it could be made to serve some useful purpose it was gladly picked up and became at once an implement. Certainly, we must believe that primitive man everywhere when he wished to attack animals or

men or to defend himself when attacked, used the first pebble
at hand and long after man had learned how to fashion all of
the various tools and weapons that his needs called for, he
still used the unworked worn pebble for a hammer, pot boiler
or tool sharpener.

Hammers

Smooth, regularly oval or round quartz pebbles furnished
excellent hammers and many of these of a pound or more weight,
are found about all village sites or even where there was once
a long occupied camp. The pecked or battered ends of such
pebbles tell the story.

Having no metal pots in which to boil their food, the
Indians used those made of earthenware and these were too
fragile to endure direct contact with the camp fire. Hence
the boiling was effected by plunging hot stones into jars
partly full of water until the water boiled. Great numbers of
these boiling stones are sometimes found about an old camp.
Of course these are merely pebbles and show no mark of use
except that in some cases the heat to which they have been
subjected has discolored them.

Figure 4 of Plate VIII shows one of the better sort of
hammer stones and figure 7 may have been a tool sharpener.

In some localities, as near Lake Bomoseen, small and flat
pebbles are found which are notched or even grooved rudely and
these are supposed to have been net or line sinkers.

Pestles.

Probably the first evolution from the hammer stone was the
pounder and then the pestle, figures 1, 2, 3 on Plate VIII.
Pounders like that seen in figure 3 are much more common in the
Ohio Valley than here. Our more common form is the much more
elaborately shaped pestle, figures 1 and 2.

These were used in pounding the corn, acorns, nuts or
whatever it might be and were often heavy and finely finished.
The largest specimen in the collection at Montpelier is eighteen inches long and nearly three inches in greatest thickness
and weighs 9 pounds. Most of the pestles, however, are somewhat smaller. Those shown on Plate 8 are less than half full
size. In the Museum at Burlington there are several large
pestles the upper ends of which are rudely, but distinctly
carved to a semblance of animal heads.

Figures 5 and 6 of Plate VIII are similar to the best
hammers but they are worked all over the surface and made very
regularly circular in form and each of the flat surfaces is
hollowed as may be seen in the figures. These were most probably used in playing certain games which are described by
the earliest explorers.

PLATE VII.

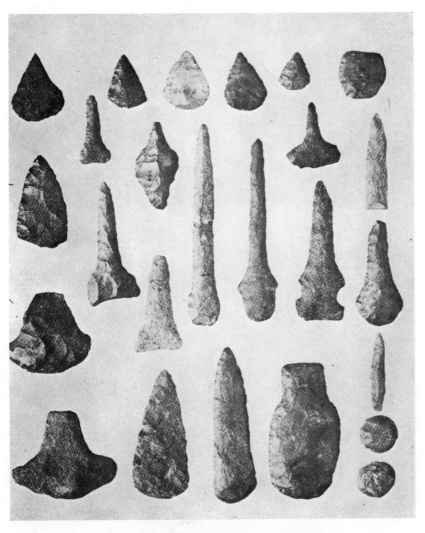

Vermont Stone Implements—Scrapers and Drills.
One-half actual size.

PLATE VIII.

Vermont Stone Implements—Pestles and Grinding Stones.
Reduced one-half.

Celts.

These implements, which in great variety of form and
size variously called chisels, hand axes or celts are more
numerous than other ground objects. The rude pebble, at first
only a hammer without any change in its shape, after awhile
was ground at one end and sharpened and then became a celt.
It probably, certainly, was used in many ways by its makers,
who having few varieties of implements were forced to use the
same for many purposes, chisel, ax, tomahawk, etc. The celts
vary endlessly in form, finish and material, but all are
longer than wide and usually narrowed at the end opposite the
edge. Plate IX shows some of those in the State collection.
Some are rude having little work put upon them except that
necessary to form the edge, others are carefully worked in
every part and some are finely smoothed or even polished.
Some are flat, others almost cylindrical. In size they vary
in length from less than three inches to ten or twelve.
Usually, the larger celts are proportionally heavy. Rarely
the celts are ground to an edge at each end and still more
rarely to a curved edge at one end, making the implement half
celt or chisel and half gouge, as in the middle left hand
figure, Plate IX. The material is commonly hard stone, green-
stone, trap, basalt, granite, etc. The amount of labor
necessary to fashion and finish one of the finer examples of
this sort must have been very great. Undoubtedly, most celts
were simply chisels or hand axes, but some we know from the
writings of early explorers were supplied with a handle. But
as the handles were of wood, no trace has remained.

We are not only told of stone axes that had handles, but
also how the handle was attached. A suitably shaped branch
was selected on some tree in the forest and this somewhat
trimmed, was cleft to receive the end of the axe but was not
cut from the tree, the axe was placed in the cleft and left
for months until the wood had grown firmly about it. Then the
branch was cut off and worked into such shape as was desired
by the maker.

The celts are usually well made and sometimes the surface
is polished, but some are rude and clumsy. None of the stone
objects found in Vermont are more finely finished than the
best of our celts. Plate IX shows a fairly good series of
the ordinary forms and shows the variation in shape and size.
Rarely, very small celts have been found, smaller than the
smallest on the plate and the largest are larger than the
longest shown.

As the skill of the makers increased, the celts were more
regularly formed, more finely smoothed. In time it was found
that a notch on each side enabled the owner to attach a handle
more securely and the straight sided celt gradually became the
notched axe. The middle figure of the left-hand row on
Plate IX shows the first step in this direction.

The notched axes occur of different sizes and with more or less deep notches until finally the notches are carried around the axe and become a groove. Thus we have,

Notched and Grooved Axes.

Plate X shows a few examples of this implement.
Apparently these were less commonly made than some other kinds of implements for, altho they are always large and of hard and enduring material, few have been found in the State. It would seem to us quite difficult, if not impossible, to cut down trees or do any very efficient work with so clumsy and dull a tool and yet they did continually use them.

Champlain, in his account of his notable first journey thru the lake to which he gave his name, that at night his savage companions cut trees with "Meschantes haches" in order to make a barricade. As Champlain says that some of the trees were large ("gros arbres") these, to us, useless tools must have been more serviceable in the hands of those who knew how to use them.

None of the Vermont axes are as large nor heavy as some found in the west. Our Vermont axes varied from little hatchets only a few inches long and weighing less than a pound, hatchets rather than axes, to those that are eight or ten inches long and several pounds in weight. On the average, the Vermont grooved axes are about seven inches long and three or four pounds in weight.

Gouges

The hollow chisel or gouge appears to be more character- istic of Vermont and to a less extent perhaps of New England than any other of our stone implements. Gouges are not unknown elsewhere, but they are neither so numerous nor so important a feature in the archeology of other regions. As a rule, the gouges are more carefully formed and perfectly finished than other stone implements. Some of them are well nigh perfect in form and finish and of handsome material. Occasionally, a rude and imperfectly finished gouge is found, but not as often as a rough celt or axe.

The same variety seen in the celts is apparent in the gouges. Hardly two are alike except in the groove and curved edge. The figures on Plate XI show examples of our Vermont gouges. It is difficult to assign a definite use to some of the gouges. While those that are made from hard rock, as most of them are, could easily have been used as gouges for all the purposes to which such an implement is adapted, some of them are of slate or even softer stone and, while these may be finished with great care and finely polished, it is certain that they could not have endured any hard usage. In length, our gouges vary from three inches or less to nineteen or twenty. Of course the weight varies with the size. The groove

PLATE IX.

Vermont Stone Implements—Celts and Axes.
One-half actual size.

PLATE X.

Vermont Stone Implements—Grooved Axes.
Reduced one-half.

PLATE XI.

Vermont Stone Implements—Gouges.
Less than one-half actual size.

PLATE XII.

Vermont Stone Amulets and Ceremonial Stones.
One-half actual size.

may extend thru the entire length or it may be confined to the edge and there are all gradations between these extremes. Most commonly the groove is excavated for several inches from the the edge and it is less common to find it passing from end to end; more rarely, as in the middle figure on the left side of Plate XI, there is a chisel edge at one end and a gouge at the other.

Like most of the figures, those on Plate XI, are somewhat less than half full size.

The long gouge in the plate is one of a number of specimens which it is difficult to account for. They are always of handsome, but rather soft stone, very carefully made and well finished, being often polished. They do not show any evidence of use. As handsome and well made as many of the so-called ceremonial stones, their shape associates them with implements and yet it is difficult to understand how they could have been designed for any use as tools when made from such comparatively soft material. Indeed, there has been considerable discussion as to the real use of any of the gouges. Nevertheless it can scarcely be doubted that most of them were used as tools. It is quite certain that fire was an important aid in excavation, as in making dug-out canoes.

The log, after being cut to the required length, was attacked with hot stones and burned in places as the workers desired, water being poured upon those parts which were not to be burned. Then the charred wood could be readily scraped away by the stone gouges. By alternate burning and scraping the work was accomplished.

Ceremonial Stones.

Plate XII shows a number of objects of various shapes and probably different uses which, for want of a more definite term, may all be classed as ornamental and ceremonial stones. Different writers have assigned various reasons for their form. They are found in every collection; are always well finished, sometimes very carefully and even elegantly; are usually different one from another, duplicate forms being rarely found in the same locality. The purpose of most of them is largely a matter of conjecture. In the upper three figures on Plate XII the first and third are of the ordinary "Banner Stone" form. Quite a number of these have been found in the Champlain Valley. All are of fine material and well made and polished. Their use is uncertain. Like some of the others, as the "One Hole and the Two Hole" stones, they may have been simply ornaments or they may have been insignia of some sort. The middle figure in the top series is one of the best of our "Two Hole" stones. The two specimens in the lower corners are examples of "One Hole" stones. These latter, it is probable, were ornaments or considered such. The conical pendant, or plummet, or sinker, seen in the middle of the left side of the plate, is more carefully finished than most specimens of

this sort and may have an ornament, but most of the objects
of this form, of which there have been quite a number found,
were most likely used as net sinkers. The discoidal stone
in the center of the plate is a form not uncommon in southern
and western localities, but very rare here. Indeed, I have
seen another Vermont specimen that compared with this in workmanship. It was found in one of the Swanton graves mentioned
above. The material is white quartz. It seems probable that
these stones were in certain games. Another form much more
rarely seen in Vermont collections than in those from other
parts of the country is the head shown at the bottom of the
plate. This and one or two others are all that have been
found in Vermont. The specimen figure, No. 7, is from a
grave in Swanton and a second, finely wrought from red slate,
was found near by. The specimen in the State collection is
made of white marble and the upper part is stained by copper
salts derived from other objects that were buried with it.

Pipes.

As everywhere, pipes are not as common as most other
classes of specimens. Still, Vermont has afforded quite a
number of excellent specimens. Several of these are shown
on Plate XIII. All of those figured are from the Champlain
Valley. These are all of stone, but earthenware pipes were
not uncommon and numerous fragments of them have been found,
but, naturally, they were more perishable than those of stone
and are more broken.

The specimens shown on Plate XIII have been selected
from a larger number and very fairly represent the general
character of our Vermont pipes. Plate XIV shows about two-
thirds natural size one of several singular stone pipes which
have been found.

Altho quite unlike the ordinary pipe in shape, this long,
tubular form is not uncommon on the Pacific Coast, and pipes
almost exactly like that figured are still used by some South
American tribes. All the specimens of this kind of pipe have
been taken from the Swanton graves, except one or two fragments. They are of stone and must have cost great labor.
The bore is small at one end and large at the other. In some
specimens a rudely made stone plug was fitted. These tubular
pipes, a dozen of which have been found in the Swanton graves,
vary in length from six to thirteen inches. The material is
a rather hard slate.

The State collection is not rich in specimens of pipes
and most of the specimens figured on Plate XIII are in the
University Museum at Burlington, but are introduced here for
the sake of completing our account. The specimens shown are
figured about two-thirds of the full size.

PLATE XIII.

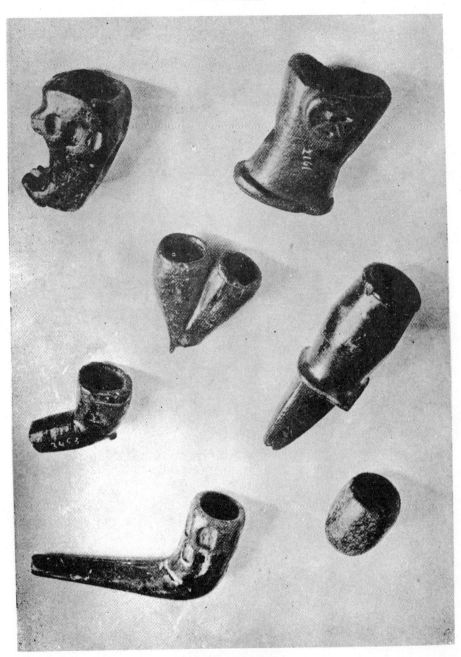

Vermont Stone Pipes.
Reduced one-half.

Plate XIV.

Tubular Pipe, Vermont.
Two-thirds actual size.

Earthenware.

Soapstone does not appear to have been extensively used for making bowls or dishes, tho it occurs in several localities in the State. Earthenware, however, was evidently very common and while made in but few shapes, was decorated in almost endless variety of pattern.

Much of the earthenware is finely made and of fine material, but there was not a little that was more simple in design and coarser in every way. The material was, in almost all specimens, a mixture of crushed granite or else the ingredients of granite, quartz, mica, feldspar and clay.

Entire jars have very seldom been found either in Vermont or anywhere in New England. So far as I know only three entire, or nearly so, jars found in this state are preserved. These are in the Museum of the University of Vermont. The material of which our pottery was made appears to have been easily broken, and while fragments are, in places, very numerous, they are only fragments. Most of our pottery is of a reddish brown color, the shade varying endlessly from light to dark and there are sometimes gray or drab pieces. Some is burned until it is black. Fortunately, the decoration was always placed about the upper part or rim, if anywhere, and it was usually confined to a limited space below the top, tho sometimes a large part of a jar was more or less ornamented. I say fortunately, because this part of all jars was made thicker, sometimes half an inch, than the rest and thus is better preserved, so that we may know more as to the patterns used than would have been possible had the more fragile parts of the jars alone been decorated.

Most of the jars made by the Indians of this region were of comparatively small size, holding from one to eight or ten quarts, but those holding twice as much have been found. In shape, nearly all are globular with a more or less constricted rim and, not infrequently, the upper third or more is made square or six-sided. In this case, the flat sides of the upper part are profusely marked with lines, dots, circles, etc.

Plate XIV shows twenty-four pieces of different patterns, shown a little less than half full size.

In thickness our pottery varies much. The smaller and finer pieces may not be more than a fifth of an inch in average thickness, except at the rim, while larger and coarser jars may be nearly half an inch thick. Pottery is far more commonly found in the Champlain Valley than in the eastern part of the state and the patterns are, some of them, Algonkin and some Iroquois. In fact, altho the Algonkins were, so far as we know, the bitter enemies of the Iroquois, who lived on the western side of the lake, they certainly either got a great deal of their pottery from them or learned many of the patterns used from them.

These patterns can not be very well described so that one who has not seen them can get a very good idea of their appearance, but some characteristic pieces are shown on Plate XV. In all the hundreds of fragments found no trace of any of the animal forms common in the mounds has been seen. Nor is there any evidence that paint or color was ever used here. All the designs, some of which are quite elaborate, were made by blunt points and variously shaped stamps on the moist surface of the clay with which all jars were coated before burning. Parallel lines in groups and slanting at various angles were most commonly used. I once counted over three hundred distinctly different patterns on a large series of fragments of rims found on the shores of Lake Champlain. Besides lines and groups of lines, there were stamped on the clay, either in rows or groups, circles, crescents, zig-zags, triangles, squares and other figures, varying not only in form, but also in size. Sometimes the effect is very pretty and in many cases the skill and regularity with which the decorating was done are remarkable.

Moreover, not only is the form of the upper part moulded in a rectangular or polygonal form, as has been notices, and thus the appearance greatly changed, but the edge of the rim is very prettily scalloped in a few specimens. In a few examples there are lines or figures on the inside for a few inches below the top. Altho, as has been noticed, we have very few entire pieces of pottery, it is not very uncommon to find bits as large as one's hand, or to find several which can be fitted to each other and thus often a considerable portion of the whole jar may be reconstructed, or could be if numerous small bits necessary to connect those present were not lacking.

Probably, many entire jars were originally buried in our soil, but because of the nature of the material from which the jars were made, as well as the freezing and thawing to which in our climate a buried jar is subjected, we now find only fragments, where under more favorable circumstances we should find whole specimens.

It is safe to say that less than a dozen entire jars found in New England are now preserved in all our collections.

Of these we have three in the University Museum at Burlington and they are larger and in some respects finer specimens than any others.

The paste from which our Vermont jars was moulded was always much coarser and more liable to injury when buried than that used either in the Mississippi Valley or the west. Nor was it often as well burned.

Less clay and more stone broken into little pieces and mixed with the clay was used here. Quartz, mica, feldspar and occasionally other sorts of stone were used. Apparently, these were mixed with more or less clay of the proper

PLATE XV.

Vermont Earthenware
One-half actual size.

PLATE XVI.

Vermont Jars of Earthenware.

consistency and the jar shaped from a mass of this, then the
whole was coated outside and usually inside, with clear clay,
thus giving the surfaces a smooth finish.

Plate XVI, b, c, d shows the three entire jars mentioned.
While we have not the real jars in the State collection, we
have exact copies of two of them made by an expert modeller
and for all ordinary purposes these are as useful as the
originals, which they exactly resemble.

The most ornate of the three, and probably none so fine
has been found in this region, was dug from under the roots
of a large tree in Colchester in 1825. Its form is peculiarly
elegant and appears to have been not very uncommon, for we
find a number of bits of rims, some of which are seen in
figure a, which evidently had a similar square form and the
decoration, lines and circles are the same on all. The
arrangement of the lines, etc., can be well seen in the
figure on Plate XVI. This jar is seven and a half inches high,
inside diameter at top, five inches, circumference around the
largest part, twenty-seven inches. When filled it holds nine
pints. Figure gives this jar one-third actual size.

A second and larger jar is that shown in Plate XVI,
figure b. This, as the figure shows, is much less decorated
and was probably a more ordinary household article. Like all
our Vermont jars, this was globular below the rim and is
ornamented only by a band of deep oblique grooves around the
thickened rim, below which is a series of deep notches. This
jar was found in Bolton about fifty years ago and was owned by
Mr. J. N. Pomeroy of Burlington, who, a few years ago, not
long before his death, gave it to the Burlington Museum. It
is nine and a half inches high, seven and a half inches in
diameter at the top and twenty inches in circumference at the
largest part. When filled it holds fourteen quarts.

The third entire Vermont jar has not yet been copied so
that we have nothing to represent it in the State collection,
but for the sake of completeness it is shown on Plate XVI,
figure c. Figures b and c are reduced to pattern more than
one-seventh of the real size of the jars.

As has been noticed above, the two other jars were discovered many years ago, but this lay unnoticed until found
in the woods by a hunter in 1895. It lay in a sort of cave-
like shelter made by large rocks that had fallen against each
other in Bolton Falls. It was bought by Dr. C. G. Andrews,
then of Waterbury, and given to the Museum at Burlington.

As the figure well shows, the general form is globular,
while the rim is hexagonal. The shape is very regular and
true. As will be seen, the ornamentation is very much like
that of the first mentioned specimen.

Decoration is confined to the upper portion, except that a lightly marked band of simple oblique lines extends around the upper part of the globular body, below the neck.

This jar is ten inches high, nine inches across the opening, thirty-six inches in circumference at the largest part and holds, when full, twelve quarts.

It should be noted that in making the plate the photographs of the jars were not reproduced uniformly, b and c are really much larger than d, tho in the plate they are smaller. This plate was loaned by the American Anthropologist.

It is extremely fortunate that our jars were made thicker and consequently, more enduring about the upper part, for here is always found the decoration. As a result of this we have a large collection of larger or smaller bits of rims and upper portions of jars and from these we learn much as to the taste of the makers and styles of decoration that otherwise would be wholly unknown. Plate XVI, figure a, shows, about one-fifth natural size, an assortment chosen from many specimens and from these some idea as to the forms, decorations, etc., of our pottery may be gained.

When we consider that all jars were made entirely by hand without the use of any wheel or other appliance, the exactness of form and general regularity seen in all the specimens is remarkable.

Not only jars, but also pipes were made of earthenware. Some of these were of finer paste and more delicate finish than was usual in the jars. Most of these were bent, that is like modern pipes, the stem at right angle with the bowl, but some were only curved and others quite straight.

Dishes of Soapstone.

Fragments of what appear to have been more or less shallow and rather clumsy bowls or dishes, each cut from a single block of stone, have sometimes been found in this State. As only a few fragments of this not easily destroyed material have been preserved, it is safe to conclude that dishes of this sort were never common. The fragments are large enough to show that none were very large. There are a few of these in the State collection.

Objects of Bone.

Until quite recently only one or two specimens made of bone had been found in Vermont. The specimen figured on Plate XVII, at the lower part of the plate, was one of the first found. This appears to be somewhat imperfect along the upper edge.

The figure, which is nearly full size, gives a better idea of the decorating by incised lines than a verbal description. The character of this specimen must be problematical. It was, most likely, some sort of an ornament, as is indicated by the care with which it is decorated. It was found near Swanton. Bits of the prongs of deer's horn have now and then been found which bear some indications, notches, grooves or worked tips of having served some useful purpose in prehistoric times, but in most cases the work shown is very little, tho sufficient, usually, to afford conclusive proof of use. They have also always been found associated with stone implements or pottery. A few years ago, however, our list of Vermont bone objects began to be materially increased. Mr. D. B. Griffin, in exploring what appeared to be an old camping place on the large creek which flows thru the western part of Colchester and empties into Malletts Bay on the northeast side, found a number of bone implements associated with the usual forms of stone points, knives, pottery, etc. The locality is not far from the bay and just beyond is a large marsh filled with cat-tails in which, for no one knows how long, muskrats have lived in large numbers. The place was admirably adapted for a camp, as it could not be seen from the lake, nor even from the bay until approached quite closely. The soil in which the objects have been found is a compact clay, most of it being under water except when the lake is low.

All the specimens figured on Plate XVII, except those at the bottom, were found here. They are shown a little less than natural size. Not all those shown are in the State collection, some being in the Nuseum at Burlington. In the upper left corner are three teeth which have been much worked. The two canines at the top are from a bear. The first has been worked down obliquely to a sharp edge. The surface is polished. The second figure shows a tooth split in halves, or else it must have been worked down until one-half was worn away. The worked surface is very smooth and carefully finished. The object below this is not very well shown. It is the incisor or gnawing tooth of a woodchuck, a part of which has been obliquely worked off so that a very sharp point and edge is left. Another rodent tooth, perhaps from a beaver, is much more worked down. It is about two inches long and only a thin portion of the outer side is left.

The three cylindrical points or perhaps awls, are very nicely worked and polished as are the two larger points shown on each side of that bearing four barbs. These are all excellent specimens of bone implements.

The curious specimen shown at the upper right hand corner appears to have been designed as a pottery marker. At least it is difficult to find another use for it. The upper end is only broken, but the lower is evenly worked and has three blunt points separated by curved edges, one of which is seen in the figure. The small spear point, having four more or

less complete barbs on each side, is the only specimen of the
sort that I have seen from Vermont, tho similar forms have been
found near Plattsburg, and on the west side of Lake Champlain.
A larger and less carefully made specimen with one barb is
whown at the right side of the plate.

Besides objects like those figured, numerous bones and
deer prongs have been found in this locality which show some
sort of notching or smoothing. Also many bones of deer, bear,
wolf, beaver and other animals and some human bones, including
nearly the whole of a skeleton. Most of these are in the
University Museum at Burlington, but a representative series
has been given to the collection at Montpelier.

Objects of Shell.

There are in the Montpelier collection a number of cylindrical beads made from shell. Two of the larger of these
are shown at the lower right hand corner of Plate XVII. Smaller beads have also been found and little shells, Marginealas,
were bored from end to end and used as beads. All of these
were found in the Swanton graves. It is an interesting fact
that these shell beads are made from southern species, such as
are not found north of the Carolinas.

Objects of Copper.

The native copper from the Lake Superior region was evidently obtained and used by the Indians of the Champlain Valley,
or they may, by trade or capture, have obtained the implements
after they were made.

Figures 1-7 of Plate XVIII show, reduced to rather less
than one-half full size, several of our copper objects. They
are nowhere common but appear to have been used in different
parts of the State, tho it is true of all classes of Indian
relics that more and finer specimens have been obtained in the
western part of the State. Figures 1 and 2 are examples of
points of which quite a number have been found in different
parts of Vermont. Some have no notched stem and may have
been simply knives.

Points having a semi-tubular half, as in figure 2, are
occasionally found, some of them large. Celts like those seen
in figures 3 and 6 are usually not large. The specimens
figured were all beaten from the native copper and are more
or less corroded.

A very large celt, which is not figured, is in the Museum
at Burlington. This is much larger than any other copper
specimen that has been found in Vermont. It is eight inches
long, two wide and weighs thirty-eight ounces. It was found
near the mouth of Otter Creek at Fort Cassin. The size, however, is not the most remarkable feature of this specimen.
While all other copper objects that we have appear to have

PLATE XVII.

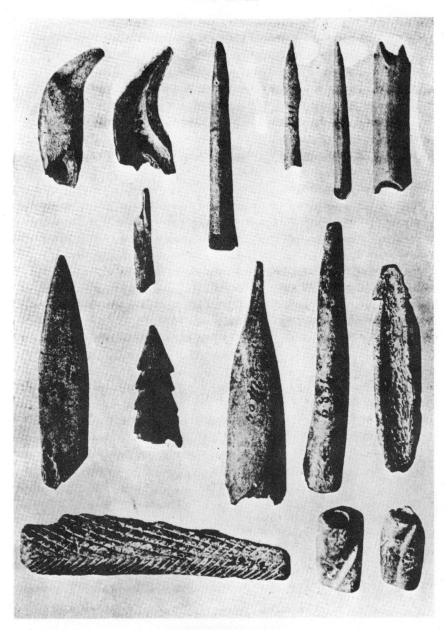

Vermont Bone Implements.
About three-fourths actual size.

PLATE XVIII.

Vermont Implements—Copper and Iron.
About one-half actual size.

appear to have been without doubt beaten into shape, this
appears to have been cast. Not only does it present a surface which shows no hammer marks, but it bears thru the
length of the upper or flat surface an irregular ridge as if
from a rude mould. Along the sides are other less continuous
ridges. The appearance is that of small, raised, irregular,
ridge-like marks as if from a rudely made mould. Altogether
this is a very interesting specimen.

A fine copper gouge was found in Milton, shown in
figure 4.

Figure 5 is one of several copper bars found in the
Swanton graves, as was also the bead, figure 7, of which a
number were found.

Objects of Iron.

When the first white men came to America the natives had
no knowledge or working iron. Now and then they picked up a
bit of meteoric iron and fashioned it into some charm or
ornament, but they could do nothing with the very abundant
ores of iron. Copper and bronze were used, but no iron.

Hence all the implements found which are of iron must
have been introduced by the white traders. That is, all iron
objects, except as indicated, date from the sixteenth century
or later. Probably those found in this region are not earlier
in origin than the latter part of the seventeenth century.

Some, of course, may be much later, still the form and
appearance of those in our museums indicate considerable age.
Figures 8-10 on Plate XVII show the more characteristic forms
of the iron implements that have been dug up. All are much
rusted and probably many have wholly perished for, while
comparatively few have been found, it seems quite certain
that many must have been used in barter with the Indians.

The Indians when trade began were eager, as all old
writers tell us, to get iron in any form, while they had no
use for money. Hence iron was the common currency for a
long time.

The most common form of trade as used in the Champlain
Valley was that shown by figure 8, Plate XVIII. These axes
were of various sizes, from those that can hardly be called
more than hatchets to full sized axes. That is, they were
from less than five to more than seven inches long and proportionally wide and thick. These axes were apparently in
common use both among those tribes which had trade with
Europeans and also the white settlers themselves. Another
less common form is that shown in figures 9 and 10 and a
still different and probably more modern form was a combination pipe tomahawk, the part above the handle being
fashioned into a pipe bowl and the handle perforated for the

stem, while below was a blade that could be used as hatchet or tomahawk. This form has persisted until now, for some of the pipes made within the last fifty years by Indians of the plains are quite similar to those that have been dug up in Vermont. Some of the modern pipes made from the red pipe stone, are also of similar shape.

It has been noticed that, while most of the objects figured on the accompanying plates are those taken from specimens in the State collection, a few have been made from objects in the Museum of the University at Burlington. Only when objects could not be well figured from the Montpelier specimens have others been taken. All are more or less reduced as has been stated.

For the benefit of special students of Vermont Arccheology it may be proper to state here that by far the most extensive and complete collection of Vermont Indian Relics that has been or that ever can be gathered together is that at the University of Vermont. This contains over fifteen thousand specimens. Nevertheless, tho small, the Montpelier collection possesses some exceedingly good representative specimens of most of the different kinds of objects of this sort that are found in this State and it is hoped that ere long all the groups will be represented in the State collection. The figures are all from photographs taken directly from the specimens.

As to the origin of the Indian relics of this State, we know pretty certainly that all, unless now and then a stray piece, came in by trade or fortune of war from outside, were made and used by Algonkin and Iroquois tribes. But when we attempt to separate our specimens into two groups, one of which represents one people and the other the other, we find ourselves quite puzzled. Of course, if we could definitely determine which of these people occupied the Champlain Valley at a given time we could be much more sure as to our conclusions, but this is not easy to do. For a very long time before the coming of the first white men the western side of the lake was inhabited solely by Iroquois tribes, but the eastern side of the lake, between it and the Green Mountains, is less certain as to its occupation. It is well known that when the first white settlers came into what is now Vermont they found the region held and more or less fully occupied by Algonkins, as was the case throughout New England, but this does not appear to have been so always, for Champlain, in his account of the discovery of the lake, says that, when in course of his journey from the large islands in the northern part, he looked at the lands and mountains to the east and asked his savage companions who lived there, they told him that they were inhabited by their enemies, the Iroquois, who had there fertile fields where they raised crops. And there is abundant evidence that Colden, the first English historian of the Six Nations, and other early writers spoke of the lake as possessed by the Iroquois. Champlain himself on his first map, published in 1612, puts down the lake as "Lac des Iroquois" and for a long time in the 17th century the Sorel was called "Riviere des Iroquois." Still, too much may not be concluded from this for in the Jesuit Relation of 1664-65 we find the statement that this name was given to the river "Because it forms the highway leading from them to us and by that route the Barbarians have most often come to attack us." It is also well known that, beginning with 1798 and repeating the claim from time to time until 1874, the Iroquois presented demands for payment for a large tract of land in western Vermont to successive Legislatures. They based their claim on the fact of original occupancy of the region.

The claim was made first in 1798 by Indians of the Caughnawaga tribe. They claimed as their long possessed hunting lands all the territory on the east side of Lake Champlain "Beginning on the east side of Ticonderoga from thence to the great falls on Otter Creek and continues the same course to the height of land that divides the streams between Lake Champlain and the river Connecticut; from thence along the height of land opposite Missisquoi and then down to the Bay." This claim was signed by twenty chiefs of several tribes.

As those familiar with Vermont geography will at once see, this claim includes the whole of the Champlain Valley. While carefully investigated by several committees appointed by the Legislature, they were not allowed. But that some foundation for them did exist is evident and the main reason for refusing to grant any of them was based upon other grounds than that the plea of former occupation was false.

The Algonkins claimed that, altho the Iroquois did possess, in Champlain's time, most of western Vermont, the land originally belonged to them and had been taken from them by their enemies who had no right to it.

In the Appendix to his History of Montpelier, pp. 303-309, Mr. D. P. Thompson discusses the "Aboriginal Inhabitants of Winooski Valley" in a very satisfactory manner and concludes by saying, "In view then of all the evidence on both sides of this question, we think we are warranted in deducing the following conclusions:-- 1st. That the Abenaki or Eastern Indians, were the original owners and the first and last possessors of the Winooski Valley and all the rest of Vermont was claimed by the Iroquois. 2nd. That the Iroquois did come in possession of this territory by conquest some short time previous to 1540 and held it and lived in it till near 1640, when they voluntarily relinquished it to the original owners, the Abenakis, who coming in, perhaps stealing in, took full possession and retained it for the next hundred years, or till the settlement of the State by our ancestors between 1740 and 1760."

From this it may be easily seen that any separation of
Algonkian and Iroquoian objects found in Vermont must be practically impossible except in some cases. Probably most of the
specimens found in eastern Vermont are to be considered
Algonkin or what is the same thing, Abenakis, for these are a
division of the Algonkins. The specimens from western Vermont
are to be regarded as in part Algonkian and in part Iroquoian.
In the forms and character of many of the stone implements
there does not seem to be much difference. In the designs on
the pottery, while there is similarity, there are differences.
Some of our pottery is of the Iroquoian stamp and some with
simpler decoration, Algonkian. Probably most of that shown in
Plate XVI is Iroquoian, as also the three entire jars.

Attention may be called in closing this account of the
collections to a very instructive series of large photographs
which are placed on the walls of the main cabinet room. A
number of marble and granite quarries are shown and from them
some idea of the nature of our quarries and the methods employed in working them may be gained.

* *

MOUND EXCAVATIONS

Persons interested in excavations of mounds (tumuli) are
referred to Smithsonian Institution Bureau of American
Ethnology Bulletin 151, (1953) especially pages 313-395 and
Plates 24-29. This work has been published also as Explo-
ration of an Adena Mound at Natrium, West Virginia, by Ralph
S. Solecki; Anthropological Papers, Number 40, Government
Printing Office, Washington, D. C., 1953.

WARNING: It is probable that no such mound or tumulus
exists as far east as Vermont.

LESLIE B. TRUAX

Undoubtedly the most thorough student of Indian Life in Vermont has passed with the death of Leslie B. Truax. As a collector of Indian relics left by the tribes which formerly inhabited the regions of northern Vermont and along the shores of Lake Champlain, Mr. Truax achieved a remarkable success. The legacy he left for history comprises some of the rarest, most perfect and most curiously interesting specimens of the handicraft of the American Indian anywhere in existence. Reginald Pelham Bolton, eminent student of the American Indian once referred to Mr. Truax as the "veteran archeologist of the upper Vermont region." There can be no doubt that he was.

His work and his study of Indian archeology extends back over sixty years and had its beginnings in the fascinating pastime of unearthing flint arrowheads from the fields in the vicinity of Swanton -- Taquahunga Falls-- as it was known in the days of the Indian, where there was said to be a larger population of Red men than there is of white folk today.

From this boyish diversion there grew the serious hobby of collecting Indian relics and a study of the habits and customs of the Lake Champlain Indian which were destined to bring to Mr. Truax an enduring fame, if not material fortune. In years gone by he prowled and explored the entire lower reaches of the Missisquoi river, he excavated former Indian camping grounds in every part of Franklin county, and he amassed several collections of perfect specimens to repay him for his lifetime of patient effort.

Mr. Truax finally came to be considered an authority on the subject of Indian relics and as such contributed many valuable and instructive articles to scientific journals. He was widely known to all museum curators and to learned scholars whose particular line of research was the habitat of the American Indian.

There is little public interest in success such as Mr. Truax achieved. Arrowheads, full-fashioned if crude, and fragments og grey and strangely decorated pottery naturally mean very little to the average individual whose chief concern lies in the problem of earning a livelihood in this modern day of automatic guns and automatic tools.

To the nature lover, to the student of early Vermont
history and to the learned scientist, however, the Truax
collections of Indian relics represent a priceless contri-
bution to the advancement of knowledge, and posterity will be
grateful for his life-time of effort and accomplishment.

THE INDIANS
by
L. B. Truax
(from St. Albans "Messenger" 1914)

While there is no possible means of knowing how long man
has existed within the territory now known as Franklin and
Grand Isle counties, yet, to any thinking investigator or
relic hunter, the fact soon becomes plain, that man existed
here for a long period. The depth at which many of the specimens are found, is alone strong proof of this fact; also the
condition of the specimens themselves.

Relics are found in many places from one to three feet
below the present surface of the soil, not stray pieces that
might by some means have been covered, but many pieces in a
strata of flint chips, bits of pottery, with traces of a dark-
er earth, the remains of one-time surface soil. Of course in
some localities the depth at which a specimen lay would be no
means of judging its age. Light sandy soil, like that upon
what is locally known in Swanton as the Hempyard, where the
earth moves and piles up like the drifting snow, might, one
season cover objects to a depth that would require centuries
in another place. But we must remember that even then the
work of the winds and storms was comparatively as nothing before the land was cleared. . . . .
But from the sum of evidence of many localities, some favorable to rapid deposit and others not, we can but decide that
man to have left his relics at the depth in the soil that they
are found, must have lived there at a time so remote that all
historic past is but a matter of today.

At West Swanton, upon the farm of A. Niles, digging for
the foundation of a barn an ancient ore-bed was discovered
about four feet below the surface, under gravel and upon the
clay, fragments of pottery. Several implements were also
found. At East Alburg, upon what is known as Fox Hill, is a
deposit of chippings, pottery fragments, fire stones, etc.,
at a depth varying from one and one-half feet to three feet.
On an interval, about two miles below the village of Swanton,
is a well defined strata of relics, at least two feet below
the surface. Several years ago a spring freshet washed away
the soil at this place for a number of rods along the river,

exposing a great quantity of chippings, pottery and implements. Of course this place is subject to an annual overflow and a deposit of alluvial, but how long a time must it have taken to make soil two feet in depth? Mention might be made of any number of such places.

That there were periods when this territory was not inhabited by any settled people is proved by history as well as by evidence from the field. In 1609, when Champlain made his voyage of discovery up the lake that bears his name, he had with him a number of Indians from the vicinity of Montreal. They were Algonquins, one of the great races that inhabited this country, made up of many tribes and occupying nearly all such territory west and south. As Champlain entered the region of the lake, his Indians were fearful of an attack from the Iroquois. This was another nation of Indians that inhabited North America, and consisted at that time of five tribes, the Mohawks, the Oneidas, the Senecas, the Cayugas and the Onondagas. In 1712 the Tuscaroras were added, and the confederacy was afterwards known as the Six Nations. They inhabited what is now the State of New York, considerable territory west of it, and part of western Vermont. They were powerful people, with a good system of confederation and wise laws, and were deadly enemies of the Algonquins. That they inhabited part of this section of country is plain from Champlain's account, vis: "I saw four beautiful islands, ten, twelve and fifteen leagues in length, formerly inhabited, but abandoned since they have been at war, the one with the other, continu - ing our route along the west side of the lake, viewing the country, I saw on the east side very high mountains capped with snow. I asked the Indians if these parts were inhabited? They answered me, yes; and that they belonged to the Iroquois, and that there were in those parts beautiful valleys, and fertile fields bearing as good corn as any I had eaten in the country, with an infinitude of other fruits." Thus the Iroquois, while inhabiting the southern portion of the State, westward of the mountains, probably had not any extensive or long continued settlement east of them, but quite likely occupied for a time the territory along the base of the Green Mountains, well to the north.

The country now comprising Franklin and Grand Isle counties, and probably part of the region along the Sorel River, was disputed territory. We find in many places in this region beds of relics, ... with an intervening period at Champlain's time was unoccupied, it belonged to the Iroquois, probably by right of conquest, their claim seemingly acceded to by the Algonquins. In 1798 the surviving representatives of the Iroquois presented a claim to the Legislature of Vermont for the payment of about two million acres of land. This claim has been presented many times since, last in 1888.

But though the Iroquois undoubtedly owned this section, they afterwards withdrew to the west of Lake Champlain; then a tribe of the Algonquin race, the "Abenaqui" came in, possibly back to their own land from which they had been driven by the Iroquois. They were the people found here by the early white settlers, and were afterwards known as the St. Francis Indians from the fact that a large number of them were at one time settled at the village of St. Francis. Their principal village seems to have been upon the banks of the Missisquoi River, and while evidence of occupation in the way of relics of every kind is abundant for many miles along its banks, the greater number are to be found about two miles below the village of Swanton, where many hundreds of specimens have been picked up. The writer alone has collected upwards of one thousand from this locality. These relics are probably in part the remains of this last race, while others were doubtless left by the Iroquois; and there is no question but that some of these relics are of a people that dwelt in this region at a period much earlier than that of the Algonquins or Iroquois.

The tribes of Abenakis, or St. Francis Indians, probably settled here about 1650, and became strong allies to the French in the early wars, seemingly bound to them by religious ties, through the efforts of the Franciscan and Jesuit priests. About 1725 these in the immediate vicinity of the village on the river left because of the fatal plague that raged among them, and settled at St. Francis, but fifteen years later they had mostly returned, and it was what the old records call "a large Indian town," which continued about the same until 1763, when a treaty of peace was signed between England and France, by which this region and the entire northeasterly possessions of the French in America were ceded to the English. The Indians, who had sided with the French in the wars of the past were not left in the hands of their enemy, and their gradual withdrawal from this territory followed. They continued to occupy, however, up to at least as late as 1800, and it is said by old inhabitants that they were in the habit of drifting back in bands of eight or ten families to favorite camping grounds to spend part of the year, up to as late as 1835 or 1840. That the Abenakis were engaged in the expedition against the infant settlements to the south is certain, as the following extracts from an old French diary preserved in the colonial history of New York gives a clear idea of the methods pursued, the French supplying an outfit to the Indians doing the work. "March 16th, 1746 -- The Abenakis went toward Boston and returned with some scalps and prisoners." "A party of twenty Abenakis set out towards Boston and returned with some scalps and prisoners." May 24 -- Party of eight Abenakis of Missiskow fitted out, went in direction of Boston, returned with prisoners and scalps." "June 12 -- Equipped party of ten Abenakis who made an attack in the direction of Boston."

It seems probable that some of the Abenakis were with the party in the expedition against Deerfield, Mass., February 29, 1704, as the Rev. John Williams, who was captured at that time, and taken by the Indians to Canada, says in his memories entitled "The Redeemed Captive Returning to Zion," that after going some distance on the ice up the lake from the mouth of the French (Onion) River, "We went a day's journey from the lake to a company of Indians who were kind to me giving me the best they had, which was moose flesh, ground nuts and cranberries." We stayed at the branch of the lake and feasted two or three days on geese that were killed there." It is likely that the "branch of the lake" was Missisquoi Bay, and that the geese were killed, and the cranberries picked in the marshes about the mouth of the river. Mrs. Jemmia Howe's captors were also Abenakis. She was taken from Vernon, Vt., in 1775, and after being held captive in this vicinity for some time, was taken to St. John's and sold to a French gentleman. She described this locality in after years very closely, particularly "the cove" about two miles above the village of Swanton.

Ancient Village Sites

There are many places in this region that bear evidence of habitation. Some of course were a mere cluster of homes, while in other places the great quantity of implements, chippings, etc., that are found, indicate large and populous towns and long continued occupancy. The result of an active investigation and study of this region, extending over a period of ten years, leads the writer to the belief that the number of people inhabiting this region in the past, has been very much underestimated by writers and students of this subject. John B. Perry the only scientist who ever gave this region a thorough investigation, must have been in error when he said in his History of Swanton: "In many localities indeed, Indian relics have been found, chips of chist, as I well remember, are met with in one place in considerable abundance." There is probably not a farm in Grand Isle county that lacks some evidence of ancient occupation, and throughout Franklin county they are nearly as abundant. For fifteen miles along the banks of the Missisquoi River, and for one and one-half miles back, there is hardly a field but upon which can be found some traces of ancient occupancy. The same may also be said of the shores of Franklin pond, and in fact the entire country. A few scattered chips and fragments of pottery of course would not mean a village site, but rather an isolated home; places where the ground is literally filled with such indications, as, for instance, many acres on the Burton farm in Swanton, seem to indicate thickly populated villages. Many other places beside this one are to be found in this region.

Implements, and Their Probable Uses

In describing the use to which an Indian implement might be put we are apt to judge from the standpoint of our own necessities, forgetting that the race that used the stone axe and spear were different from ourselves and under different conditions of life, and that their needs were not our needs.

Taking relics in classes, the arrow point, is the first to attract attention, both by reason of number and importance. These are found in abundance throughout this entire region, and are too familiar an object to require either illustration or description. The material used in making the arrow-head is generally some of the varieties of quartz, yet arrowpoints of slate are occasionally found either chipped or worn into form and sometimes one is found made of copper. All the usual forms are found in this region, the surated, or barbed point, being the rarest. The writer knows of but one typical specimen of that variety being found here. The arrow point was probably one of the most useful implements primitive man had, it being his dependence in both the chase and war.

THE TRUAX COLLECTION
by

Horace Eldred   January 21, 1935

A short time ago the Fleming Museum came into possession of the largest privately owned collection of Vermont Indian material in existence. This collection is the result of the long-continued, intelligent exploration and excavation of the Mississquoi region by the late L.B. Truax of St. Albans. Mr. Truax was untiring in his endeavors to add native Vermont material to the rapidly filling shelves in his cabinets. This characteristic in addition to his method of carefully marking each specimen with its locality made the Truax collection one which was known far and wide and visited by many. Some came from curiosity to see how many worthless stones an otherwise normal man would gather in his house, while others came with reverence for another's hobby or interest in Indian lore of Vermont. They were well repaid in seeing this collector lovingly handle and almost caress each specimen as he would carefully tell of the circumstances surrounding the discovery of every individual object.

I knew Mr. Truax very well and gathered much useful knowledge from him during many hours together. This occurred during his several visits to the old University Museum.

He was a rather small man but very spry for his years. With his gray hair, van dyke beard, large glasses and ever present pipe, he was a person to arouse interest even before you learned of his knowledge of Vermont Indian lore which he had accumulated during a period of over sixty years.

In the case of Mr. Truax, the Museum policy of not opening exhibition cases for visitors was ignored. A great number of the Museum relics were fondly handled and discussed. The different methods of manufacture of the specimens and their possible uses were thoroughly investigated, for a single question from me would draw a full discussion from Mr. Truax. During many subsequent visits the procedure was the same, not only the opening of cases and discussions but at times a complete repetition of the details concerning material gone over before. But in the true manner of an enthusiast talking about his hobby each repetition was as energetically and completely given as the first, and received in the same manner.

Such was the man who untiringly hunted over each piece of ground in Franklin County, especially the Mississquoi region, while from his long experience he deducted the village sites, trading posts and individual camps of this locality.

Any collection of Indian relics is dominated by an abundance of arrow points and the Truax material is no exception. Of the some two thousand specimens, 645 are arrow points exhibiting the importance of this article to the Indian. From the great variety of patterns in the so-called arrow points and spear heads the conclusion has been reached by archeologists that the several patterns were designed not for one, but many purposes. One of these patterns resembles a very blunt arrow point and could be fastened to a stout stick in the manner of an arrow point and used to scrape skins. Another pattern has the regular stem of most arrow points, sometimes notched, but very slender in the main part. This type was used for drilling holes through pendants and other stone objects.

Many of the spear head type were used as knives, some being fastened to wooden handles. Some of the knives are semi-lunar in shape but practically anything with a sharp edge would be used as a knife. Axes, mauls, gouges, tubes, celts and pendants are all represented here.

I wish at this time to draw on some material written about the Truax collection by Mr. Ira A. Manley, son-in-law of Mr. Truax. Mr. Manley has a large collection of Indian relics most of which he discovered himself and is familiar with the territory where Mr. Truax found most of the material. In part he says:

"The collection of Indian relics and artifacts of the
late L.B. Truax is considered the most complete of any private
collection in Vermont. Most of these specimens were found in
Franklin County which in early times was 'No Man's Land' for
Iroquois and Algonquin Indians. The French and English fought
over and occupied it for varying lengths of time.

"The most interesting group of artifacts in the collection is that found on the Frink grounds in St. Albans.
This is known as the 'Red Paint Cemetery' -- so called from
the amount of red ochre in the graves and the condition of the
soil around the graves. Two specimens from one of these
graves are stone tubes, six and ten inches long by one inch or
more in diameter. These are regarded by some people as musical
instruments. A perforated w s stone, several dozen arrow
points, spear points and knives complete the list of this group.
So far this is the only known cemetery of the red paint people
in Vermont and comparatively little is known about this early
race.

"Another fertile field for exploration was the valley of
the Mississquoi where several thousand specimens were found.
Every spring during high water and the breaking up of the ice,
the banks of the river and adjoining lands are left barren
and broken, thus exposing many interesting relics.

"An unusual feature of this territory is the amazing
variety of objects ranging all the way from tiny bird points
to unwieldly mining implements of the chert quarry. All
varieties of stone capable of being chipped were used and many
ground and polished specimens are found.

"This chert quarry, before mentioned, lies about two
miles northwest of St. Albans Bay on which is known as the
Brooks farm. Here students of Indian life may observe all
the details of mining and quarrying as carried on by the early
inhabitants of this region.

"This process in brief consisted of digging pits in the
ground as near as possible to a ledge of chert, undermining a
part if possible, and by using large stones, either thrown or
wielded as mauls, portions large and small were broken off.
These pieces were then reworked, according to their adapta-
bility, into the various implements of war or agriculture.

"Nearer the lake and along the marshy land southeast of
the 'Quarry' lies what is known as the 'Deposit' where much
of the Quarry material is found buried or cached either for
preservation or transportation at a later date. Along with

thin cached material were many objects of seemingly different culture such as gouges, celts and finely wrought arrow points. These varying types are the cause of much speculation as to the nature of the 'Deposit.'"

In regard to the tubes mentioned there are several explanations as to their use; the one before mentioned is a possibility and under this would come its use as a moose call. But it is possible that the medicine men may have used them in drawing pain or sickness from a patient. By placing the large end over the location of the pain and sucking on the small end the pain was supposed to be drawn out. The last explanation is that they are pipes. These tubes are similar to but larger than a pipe described as being used in a ceremonial in honor of Captains Lewis and Clarke. This was of an oval form with the bowl in the same line as the stem. A small piece of burnt clay was placed at the bottom of the bowl to separate the tobacco from the stem; this was an irregular piece, not fitting the tube perfectly in order to let the smoke pass.

The Red Paint Graves mentioned by Mr. Manley require further explanation. The graves of these ancient peoples are quite numerous in Maine but as has been said are very scarce in Vermont. Mr. W.R. Moorehead in his book, Prehistoric Implements, states that the materials taken from the Red Paint Graves in Vermont are quite superior to those from Maine.

The manner of burial of these peoples was to dig a bowl shaped hole, place red ochre in the bottom next the flexed body of the deceased with his belongings, and after the grave was filled with gravel, an immense and long-burning fire was made on the grave.

The Deposit before mentioned was supposed to be a trading post where other tribes of Indians could barter for arrow point material.

Mr. Truax knew a great deal about the history of this section of Vermont and wrote many articles for publication; since this is a talk about his collection, we can do no better than to let him tell the story in his own words.

"That there were periods when this territory was not inhabited by any settled people is proved by history, as well as evidence from the field. In 1609, when Champlain made his voyage of discovery up the lake that bears his name, he had with him a number of Indians from the vicinity of Montreal. They were Algonquins, one of the great races that inhabited this country, made up of many tribes and occupying nearly all such territory west and south. As Champlain entered the region

of the lake his Indians were fearful of an attack from the
Iroquois. This was another nation of Indians that inhabited
North America, and consisted at that time of five tribes,
the Mohawks, the Oneidas, the Senecas, the Cayugas and the
Onondagas. In 1712 the Tuscaroras were added, and the confederacy was afterwards known as the Six Nations. They (the
Six Nations) inhabited what is now the State of New York,
considerable territory west of it, and part of western Vermont.
They were powerful people, with a good system of confederation
and wise laws, and were deadly enemies of the Algonquins.
That they inhabited part of this section of the country is
plain from Champlain's account, viz: "I saw four beautiful
islands, ten, twelve, and fifteen leagues in length, formerly
inhabited, but abandoned since they have been to war, the one
with the other. Continuing our route along the west side of
the lake, viewing the country, I saw on the east side very
high mountains capped with snow. I asked the Indians if these
parts were inhabited? They answered me, yes: and that they
belonged to the Iroquois, and that there were in those parts
beautiful valleys, and fertile fields bearing as good corn as
any I had eaten in the country, with an infinitude of other
fruits."

"Thus the Iroquois, while inhabiting the southern portion of
the State, westward of the mountains, probably had not any
extensive or long continued settlement east of them, but quite
likely occupied for a time the territory along the base of the
Breen Mountains, well to the north.

    "But, though the Iroquois undoubtedly owned this section,
they afterwards withdrew to the west of Lake Champlain. Then
a tribe of the Algonquin race, the 'Abenaqui' came in, possibly
back to their own land from which they had been driven by the
Iroquois. They were the people found here by the early white
settlers, and were afterwards known as the St. Francis Indians,
from the fact that a large number of them were at one time
settled at the village of St. Francis. Their principal village
seems to have been upon the banks of the Missisquoi River, and
while evidence of occupation in the way of relics of every
kind is abundant for many miles along its banks, the greater
number are to be found about two miles below the village of
Swanton, where many hundreds of specimens have been picked up.
The writer alone has collected upwards of one thousand from
this locality. These relics are probably in part the remains
of this last race, while others were doubtless left by the
Iroquois; and there is no question but that some of these
relics are of a people that dwelt in this region at a period
much earlier than that of the Algonquins or Iroquois.

    "The tribes of Abenakis, or St. Francis Indians, probably
settled here about 1650, and became strong allies to the
French."

TRUAX COLLECTION

Pendants 30

Sinkers. 1

Gouges 17

Pipes. 4

Celts. 115

Tubes. 2

Knives 214

Axes 24

Drills 6

Arrow Points 812

Scrapers 20

Pounders, Hammers, Stones. . . .39

Paint Stones 9

Miscellaneous. 27

Pestles. 7

Large Hammer 1

Anvil Stone. 1

Spear Points 44

Sinew Stone. 1

Banner Stone 1

Rubbing Stone. 1

Bird Stones. 2

Bone perforator. 1

Pottery Fragments. 54

Nest of round stones 17

Wampum

KNIVES

  6 Highgate
45
93 F.Co.
24 St. Albans
 2 Chittenden
 1 Enosburg
 5 Addison C.
 8 Swanton
 1 Georgia

181

ARROW POINTS

118
  5 Addison Co.
451 F. Co.
  7 Chittenden Co.
 33 St. Albans
 16 Swanton
 10 Highgate
  5 Georgia

645

HAMMER STONES POUNDERS

10
11 F. Co.
 4 St. Albans
 1 Highgate
 1 Swanton
 1 Chittenden

28

PAINT STONES

15
 2 St. Albans
 1 Highgate

18

PESTLES

1
5 F.C.
1 St. Albans

7

PENDANTS

25
 1 Highgate
 3 F. Co.

29

AXES

3
3 St. Albans
1 Highgate
13 F.C.

20

SCRAPERS

7
7 F.Co.
1 Swanton

15

CELTS

1
81 F. Co.

82

Drills -- 5 -- F. Co.

Spear Points -- 33 -- F. Co.

Sinew Stone -- 1 F. Co.

Gouges -- 18 -- F. Co.

Bird Stones -- 2 -- Swanton

Pipes -- 4

Tubes -- 2 -- Highgate

AXES GOUGES CELTS

```
  4
  3 St. Albans
  1 Highgate
112 F.C.
120      1 p. -- 5 -- 20 ps.
              yellow
```

DRILLS SCRAPERS PENDANTS

```
 32
 15 F. C.
  1 Swanton
  1 Highgate
 49      1 p. -- 5 -- 10 ps.
              Blue
```

KNIVES SPEAR POINTS

```
 45
  6 Highgate
126 F. Co.
 24 St. Albans
  2 Chittenden Co.
  1 Enosburg
  5 Addison
  8 Swanton
  1 Georgia
218      1 p. -- 5 -- 44 ps.
              Green
```

HAMMER STONES POUNDERS PESTLES

```
 11
 16 F.C.
  5 St. Albans
  1 Highgate
  1 Swanton
  1 Chittenden C.
 45      1 p. -- 5 -- 9 ps.
              Purple
```

ARROW POINTS

```
118
  5 Addison Co.
451 F. Co.
  7 Chittenden Co.
 33 St. Albans
 16 Swanton
 10 Highgate
  5 Georgia
645      1 p. -- 10 -- 65 ps.
              Red
```

PAINT STONES

```
 15
  2 St. Albans
  1 Highgate
 18      1 p. -- 1.  orange
```

PIPES TUBES

```
  4
  2 Highgate
  6      1 p. -- 1 Black
```

Miscellaneous - white - 6

```
Sinew Stone -- 1 -- F.C.        Red
Bird Stones -- 2 -- Swanton     Blue
Banner  Stone -- 1              Yellow
Rubbing Stone -- 1              Green
Bone perforator -- 1            Orange
                                Purple
                                Black
                                White
```

Title of Article: "A Stratified Rock Shelter in Vermont"
Name of Author: Bailey, John H.
Name of Periodical: Proceedings of the Vermont Historical
                      Society, New Series, Vol. VIII, No. 1,
                      March 1940, pages 3-30.
Salient Features: In June, 1938, the Champlain Valley
    Archaeological Society was notified that a long, shallow
    rock shelter at Chipman's Point, Town of Orwell, Addison
    County, Vermont, was available for investigation. Ex-
    cavation began in July 1938; animal bones, rattlesnake
    bones, the skeleton of an eighteen year old girl, a dog's
    skeleton and various stone artifacts were found. Several
    bone implements and some pottery sherds also came to light.

            "So in the case of most rock shelters
    in this region (see Bailey: A Rock Shelter at Fort
    Ticonderoga) we have scant material evidence for deter-
    mining the cultural affinities of the people who lived
    here."

            Illustrations include a map, a photo-
    graph of "Curse Point," several diagrams, and photographs
    of materials mentioned above.

Title of Bulletin: A Rock Shelter at Fort Ticonderoga, N. Y.
Name of Author: Bailey, John H.
Publisher, etc.:   Champlain Valley Archaeological Society,
                    Fort Ticonderoga, N. Y. Vol. I, No. 1,
                    Dec. 1937.
Salient Features: Sixteen (16) pages, five (5) illustrations,
    describing in situ burial, objects from site, ground plan
    of rock shelter.

            "The shelter was formed by a projecting
    layer of limestone which extends a maximum distance of
    four feet at the present time (1937) and to some extent
    covers about eighteen feet of the floor. This....was
    evidently enough for the aboriginal inhabitants of the
    shelter at the time of their occupancy."

            Antler, bone, chipped stone, polished
    stone, pottery and human skeletal material were found
    in this overhand in Ticonderoga, N. Y., a few miles
    west of Shoreham, Vt.

Title of Article: "An Analysis of Iroquoian Ceramic Types"
Name of Author: Bailey, John H.
Publisher: American Antiquity, Volume 3, No. 4,
                   April 1938, pages 333-338.
                   (Reprinted for the Champlain Valley
                   Archaeological Society, 1938.)
Salient Features: Description of general features of Iroquoian
    pottery; design relationship between prehistoric and
    recent pottery; influences of and upon non-Iroquoian
    pottery. Three (3) illustrations from Broome and
    Livingston Counties, N. Y.

    See also MacNeish, Richard S., "Iroquois Pottery Types";
    and Winternberg, W. J., "Distinguishing Characteristics
    of Algonkian and Iroquoian Cultures," etc.

* *

    Some Archaeological Publications in the Northeast.

1.   Researches and Transactions of the New York State
      Archaeological Association. Annually. Address -
      Dr William A. Ritchie, Secretary, New York State
      Museum, Albany 1, New York.

2.   Bulletin of the Archaeological Society of Connecticut.
      Address- Dr. Irving Rouse, Yale Peabody Museum, New
      Haven, Connecticut.

3.   Bulletin of the Massachusetts Archaeological Society.
      Address- Dr. William S. Fowler, Secretary, Bronson
      Museum, North Main Street, Attleboro, Massachusetts.

THE COLONIAL
TICONDEROGA

Prehistoric Indian burial in floor of rock shelter on shore of
Lake Champlain. The skeleton shows unmistakeable evidence of
advanced stages of arthritis.

(Bailey's article; photograph by courtesy of William A. Ross)

Rock shelter at Fort Ticonderoga on shore of Lake Champlain
before excavating.

(Bailey's article; photograph by courtesy of William A. Ross)

1 Bone awls; 2 Flakers; 3 Bone drills; 4 Bone harpoon points; 5 Bone arrow heads; 6 Bone fish hooks; ?? Stone sinkers?; 7 Stone drill; 8 Pottery fragments; 9 Stone arrow heads.

Specimens from Ticonderoga rock shelter burial

(Bailey's article; photograph by courtesy of William A. Ross)

AN ABORIGINAL CHERT QUARRY IN NORTHERN VERMONT

by Reginald Pelham Bolton

Reprinted from Indian Notes, Vol. VII, No. 4,
Museum of the American Indian, Heye
Foundation, New York, October, 1930.

At the courteous invitation of Mr. L. B. Truax, the
veteran archeologist of the upper Vermont region, and accompanied by his associate, Mr. Benjamin Fisher, I was enabled to visit the extensive deposit and quarry of chert in
the vicinity of St. Albans, which was referred to in my
article on "Indian Remains in Northern Vermont."

The explanations of the two explorers and their intimate
acquaintance with local aboriginal conditions afforded an un-
equaled opportunity for understanding the significance of the
circumstances under which the quarry was worked by natives.

The outcrop of chert occurs between beds of slate in a
low ridge extending north and south for more than a mile a-
cross meadow lands bordering Lake Champlain, and it evidently
continues under the bed of the lake, for it makes a reappear-
ance on some of the nearby islands.

The chert in its original bed where it is not exposed to
the atmosphere or where it has been buried under the soil, is
dark in color, but where it is exposed it has become lighter
and on long exposure has hardened and has become a whitish
gray.

Along this ridge for a distance of about three-fifths of
a mile an immense amount of work was done in aboriginal times
in undercutting the projections of chert and removing the
slate which had overlaid the irregular course of the vein.
Large quantities of slate have been cast away in heaps sloping
from both sides of the ridge. Here and there pits are to be
traced, now nearly filled with washed-in debris. These seem
to have been dug down on some exposure of the chert, which in
some places shows its fracture by blows which have been de-
livered from above. The method thus employed is demonstrated
by many heavy hammerstones which are to be seen around the
working places, consisting of boulders or field stones, showing signs of their use, grooved, cut, and spalled on one end.
Several of these were found to be pecked on the sides so as
to afford a grip by the hands, and others are slightly grooved
around the middle, evidently for the attachment of a handle.

The fractured rock in spalls and splinters is scattered
widely along the ridge. Fragments and blocks of chert were
observed in plowed fields near by, and others were seen on
the margin of the lake half a mile away, some of which may
have been spilled or dropped during their transportation to

the water, while others have been subjected to reworking.

There are indications of intermittent mining of the vein. In some places masses of quarried slate have buried previous excavations. Old weathered exposures have been reopened, attacked, and broken. But the operations along the quarry were not confined to the extraction of blocks of the stone. In a number of places there are abundant remains of the process of flaking the material into definite shapes. Such areas are covered with flakes and spalls, and among them are easily distinguished the forms of the objects which the ancient workers were developing.

These were leaf-shape blades of varying sizes, many of which in complete or almost perfect form have been found by my genial guides, and numbers of them more or less defective are still scattered on the ridge and around the vicinity.

Nor are there lacking evidences of the method by which this part of the work was accomplished. The crude tools found with the roughed-out blades show that the system employed was flaking by percussion. Hammerstones bearing marks of use are easily found, as well as lapstones and hand-stones, both being of softer kinds of fieldstone. Some of the lap-stones have been deeply scored by the material which was held on edge upon their surfaces. The same indications are visible on some of the little split pebbles which are neatly suited to be held in the palm of the hand to receive the blow of the hammerstones.

Careful examination of all parts of the work failed to disclose any signs of the use of fire. From evidences we may judge how the work proceeded. The workmen labored hard at the strenuous work of exposing and undercutting the vein, while others raked away the soil, the spalls, and the chips with rude hoe-shape implements made of the chert, of which several were found in broken condition.

The quarrymen then with the heavy mauls and boulders pounded off large fragments of the exposed vein of chert which others carried over to the working places where the flaking and shaping process was carried on. Seated on the ground, each with a large flat-topped stone in his lap, these workers roughed out the blocks into desired shapes. These were then passed to other workers who, with a split stone in one hand, struck the edges with small hammerstones, reducing the blocks to the desired leaf-shape. They cast away such of the partly-formed blades as developed flaws or showed the existence of veins or inferior material, which castaway objects, with thousands of flakes, piled up around them. For the greater part these productions have lain buried under the accumulation of wastage, and thus retain their original color, while those which happened to be exposed on the surface have weathered to a depth greatly varying in many specimens. This depth of weathering indicates some relative age of the worked specimens, and taken into consideration with the extent of the operations of quarrying and the irregular development of the quarry, may indicate successive workings of the quarry over long intervals of time.

At the foot of the slope of quarry debris the explorers reported some places where chips and flakes indicated that some of the rough leaf-shape blades had been reqorked and shaped, but over the quarried area such reflaking or second-ary chipping of the quarried product is not apparent.

The story of the quarry presents itself as a record of systematic and laborious effort to secure a supply of the coveted material. Its output was mainly in roughly blocked-out, leaf-shape objects, all of one general form, which is in-dicative of a trading purpose. A number of these were purpose-ly buried and many were found by Mr. Truax in a large cache in a nearby place. These may have been hidden in fear of an attack by other tribes, or more probably were buried to keep them from weathering and hardening. Whatever was done with these blades does not appear on the quarry site. They were evidently traded away or carried elsewhere for the purpose of being reworked into other desired forms.

The possession of such a source of supply must have been of immense and practical value to the Indians who controlled this site. May we not read in that conclusion a possible cause of some of the tribal conflicts which afflicted the natives of this region?

Name of Article: "Indian Remains in Northern Vermont"
Name of Author: Bolton, Reginald Pelham
Name of Volume: Indian Notes, Vol. VII, No. 1, published
                  by the Museum of American Indian, New York,
                  January 1930. Pages 57-69.

Salient Features: Prominent mention of Truax Collection, with
     pictures of potsherds, stone tubes, flint fish hooks,
     an earthenware pipe; also picture of steatite pipe bowl
     at the University of Vermont.
     (Much of the text is found in the section on the Truax
     Collection, this work.)

Title of Article: "Searching for Indian Relics in Vermont"
Parts I and II
Name of Author: Bostock, Allen K.
Name of Periodical: Vermont History Magazine, Vol. XIII,
No. 3, July 1955. Vol. XIII, No. 4,
October, 1955.

Salient Features: Mr. Bostock gives interesting accounts
of his searchings and findings, especially stressing his
Folsom Point. He gives deserved praise to Professor
George H. Perkins, Dr. Warren K. Moorehead, L. B. Truax,
William A. Ross, Mr. Thomas Daniels and others who have
delved in Vermont fields.

He recommends new, scientific digs in
Swanton, Burlington, Orwell, Pittsford, Vergennes,
Colchester Point, Lake Bomoseen, and in the Connecticut
Valley. He concludes with this statement:

"I do feel that it is worth the effort,
time, and whatever it may cost to find out as much as we
can about the way they (Proto-historic and Pre-historic
Indians) lived and where, and to what extent, in our
state (of Vermont)."

See Huden, J. D.: "Indian Groups in
Vermont"; Vermont History Magazine, Vol. XXVI, No. 2,
April 1958. (Also in this work.)

* *

NATIVE AMERICAN BURIALS

Flexed burials; stone-lined graves; inclosures in mounds;
burials in caves, and brief discussion of New England Algonkian
groups are found in Bulletin 70, 1920, Smithsonian Institution
Bureau of American Ethnology by David I. Bushnell, Jr.
Full title, Native Cemeteries and Forms of Burial East of the
Mississippi. This book has 160 pages, 16 plates, an 8-page
bibliography and a 4-page index. It should be used in connection with Willoughby's Antiquities mentioned elsewhere in
this work.

Name of Article: "How Old Is It?"
Name of Authors: Briggs, Lyman J. and Weaver, Kenneth F.
Name of Magazine, etc.: The National Geographic Magazine

                        Volume CXIV No. 2, pages 234-255
                        Washington, D. C., August 1958.

Salient Features: Profusely and cleverly illustrated,
    this article is one of the best expositions of "how to
    estimate the age of objects by means of radioactive
    carbon" ever to appear in print.

    "Chemistry, Physics and Electronics combine their skills
    to date carbon"

    "Carbon dates the Ice Age"

    "Early man comes to America"

    "Radio carbon says men armed with stone tipped spears
    were hunting mammoth, bison, horse and tapir in Arizona
    at least by 10,000 B. C."

    "Carbon reaches back 70,000 years"

    (See also Ritchie, William A., "Traces of Early Man in
    the Northeast" and "A Probable Paleo Indian Site in
    Vermont" in this work.)

    (See also Sargent, Howard R., "Radio Carbon Dates and
    Their Bearing on New Hampshire Archaeology" in this work.)

Title of Article: "The Indian Fort at Lochmere, New
                        Hampshire"
Name of Author: Brown, Percy S.
Name of Periodical: The New Hampshire Archaeologist,
                        Number 3, May 1952.

Salient Features: Documentary evidences from local histories
    are quoted in support of legends concerning a stone fort
    in Sanbornton, New Hampshire; maps; diagrams.

                        This work is chiefly valuable as an
    example of high-class "detective work" leading to archaeo-
    logical investigation.

Title of Pamphlet: Proposed Artifact Classification for
                     Identification Purposes
Name of Author: Burtt, J. Frederic, Chairman, Artifact
                     Committee, New Hampshire Archaeological
                     Society. (Date of issue, July 1956.)

Salient Features: This ten (10) page dittoed, 8 1/2 x 11
     bulletin contains valuable material for the identification
     and classification of artifacts such as arrow points,
     spear points, gouges, grooved axes, notched axes, orna-
     ments, pestles, drills, scrapers, knives and banner stones.

          See also Fowler: Preliminary Classifi-
     cation Outlines, Massachusetts Archaeological Society,
     Attleboro, Mass., 1948.

Title of Article: "Algonkian Culture and Use of Maize in
                     Southern New England"
Name of Author: Butler, Eva L.
Name of Periodical: Bulletin of the Archaeological Society
                     of Connecticut, Number 22, December 1948,
                     pages 3-39.
Salient Features: Description of corn in New England at time
     of contact; annual cycle and seasonal removals; planting
     implements; fertilizers; companion crops; harvest;
     storage; uses; utensils for cooking corn; pottery; mortars
     and pestles; woodware; uses of cornhusks.

          All of this bulletin is interesting. Its
     chief value for Vermont archaeology is probably in the
     artifacts used for planting, harvesting, and cooking the
     maize.

          The bibliography (five pages) ranges
     from Jacques Cartier 1534 to Charles Willoughby's (which
     see) 1935 opus Antiquities of the New England Indians.

Title of Article: "The Mohawk Iroquois"
Name of Author: Carse, Mary Rowell
Name of Periodical: Bulletin of the Archaeological Society
                     of Connecticut, Number 23, June 1949;
                     pages 3-53.
Salient Features: History of Mohawk contacts; Mohawk culture;
     Mohawks in Canada (and by implication in Northwestern
     Vermont.) Also houses, canoes, pottery, agricultural
     implements, weapons, False Face rituals, adornment.

          On page 48 there is an excellent graphic
     chart showing persistence of Mohawk traits. The bibli-
     ography takes up four (4) pages.

          (See also Ritchie, Wm. A.: The Pre-
     Iroquoian Occupation of New York State, Rochester Museum,
     Rochester, N. Y., 1944, and his New York State Museum
     Educational Leaflets.)

Title of Bulletin: "Preliminary Classification Outlines"
                      (A proposed artifact classification
                      etc.)
Name of Author: Fowler, William S.
Publisher: The Massachusetts Archaeological Society,
                      Bronson Museum, Attleboro, Mass.
Salient Features: "The material contained in this special
     number (1958) is composed of extracts from previously pub-
     lished articles and is an answer to the continued demand"
     for such outlines.

          "It must always be kept in mind that a
classification is simply a tool devised to assist in the
orderly arrangement and in the intelligible discussion of
artifacts."

          This thirty-six page booklet is carefully
and cleverly illustrated. By means of this and the Burtt
dittoed material (see above) even an amateur can make
defensible classifications of arrow points, spear points,
knives, drills, gouges, scrapers, tomahawks, axes, pipes,
hatchets, clubs, cornplanters, hoes, and even fluted points.
There are brief comments on wing weights and pottery.

Title of Article: "Sweet-Meadow Brook: A Pottery Site in
                      Rhode Island"
Name of Author: Fowler, Wm. S.
Name of Publication: Report of the Narragansett Archaeological
                      Society, October 1956
Salient Features: By means of the grid system, a site near
     Apponaug, Rhode Island, was carefully excavated.   Stone
     hearths, refuse pits and burials were located; radio-
     carbon datings of around 1100 A. D. were noted.

          Stone bowls, stone pipes, bone imple-
ments and stone implements were collected.

          "Sometime before 1600 A. D. when pots
received their final adornment as inspired by Mohawk-
Iroquoian contacts, this site was abandoned. Evidently
this site was not occupied by Narragansetts during
historic times."

          (It is altogether possible that similar
sites might be found in the Connecticut valley towns of
Vernon, Brattleboro, Bellows Falls, Weathersfield,
Newbury and Barnet, Vermont.)

Title of Book: <u>Ten Thousand Years in America</u>
Name of Author: Fowler, William S.
Publisher: Vantage Press, New York, 1957

Salient Features: "To thos immigrants out of Asia, who dis-
     covered and settled in this country thousands of years
     before Columbus, who have earned the right to be called
     Americans."

          Chapters bearing on archaeology include
Caribou hunters; At the quarry; In the home; The potter
and her ware; Miracle maize; Wings over the sea.

          The book is well illustrated with pictures,
graphs and diagrams. The bibliography covers two pages;
there is no index.

          Considering the discovery of very ancient
artifacts in northern Vermont this book helps to il-
luminate the questions "Where did the Indians come from?
How did they get here? How long ago?"

* *

DIGGINGS AT FORT STE. ANNE
ISLE LA MOTTE

     According to the Edmundite Fathers, a certain Father
Kerlidou was in charge of Fort Ste. Anne at Isle La Motte
some half century ago. On Saturdays Father Kerlidou would
adjourn his catechism classes and have the children search
systematically in several old cellars of the Fort, which was
established by the French in the 1660's.

     Father Kerlidou's religion classes apparently unearth-
ed a considerable amount of mixed French and Indian materials,
some of which are still on display in the Shrine Museum.

Title of Ph.D. Thesis: <u>Early Geography of Champlain Lowland</u>
Name of Author: Jackson, Eric Pearson
Institution: The University of Chicago Department of Geography
              Chicago, 1929
Salient Features: Chapter I, Indian Highways; Chapter II,
    The Champlain Lowland; Chapter III, Indian Activities
    as Related to the Natural Environment.

        There are one hundred and five (105) illustrations,
twenty-four (24) plates and a bibliography of fifteen
(15) pages.

        The book is eight and three quarters inches (8 3/4)
wide, eleven and one half (11 1/2) inches long and one
and one half (1 1/2) inches thick. The text is typed on
letter size paper.

        Dr. Jackson drew heavily on the works of Professor
George H. Perkins, especially the material in the 1910
report of Vermont's State Geologist, which is featured
in this compilation.

Title of Article: "Mountains and Aborigines of Champlain
                   Lowland"
Name of Author: Jackson, Eric Pearson
Periodical: Appalachian, Old Series
             Vol. 24, pp. 121-136
The material in this article appears in part in <u>Early
Geography of Champlain Lowland</u>, which see.

Title of Article: "Indian Occupation of Champlain Lowland"
Name of Author: Jackson, Eric Pearson
Periodical: Michigan Academy of Science, Arts and Letters,
             <u>Papers</u>, Vol. 14
The material in this article appears also in <u>Early
Geography of Champlain Lowland</u>, which see.

STATE OF MINNESOTA

Archaeological Laws

84.37 RIGHT OF EXPLORATION RESERVED BY STATE:-

The State of Minnesota reserves to itself the exclusive
right and privilege of investigating, exploring, excavating
and surveying, by and through the persons it may license
for that purpose, all aboriginal mounds and earthworks,
ancient burial grounds, prehistoric ruins, fossil bone deposits, and other archaeological and vertebrate paleonto-
logical features within the state, subject to the rights of
the owners of any privately-owned lands upon which the same
may be situated, to use such lands for agricultural, domestic,
or industrial purposes, and the ownership of the State is
hereby expressly declared in any and all articles, antiques,
fossil remains, implements, or material found or discovered
by virtue of such investigating, exploring, excavating or
surveying. (1939c. 207s.1) (3109-1)

DOES <u>VERMONT</u> NEED
SUCH   A   LAW?

Title of Bulletin: "Iroquois Pottery Types, a Technique
                      for the Study of Iroquois Prehistory"
Name of Author: MacNeish, Richard S.
Publisher: National Museum of Canada, Ottawa, Canada
                      (National Museum Bulletin Number 124,
                      1952)

Salient Features: Because northwestern Vermont was for
    many years controlled by the Iroquois, and some of the
    best specimens of Iroquoian pottery have been found in
    Vermont, Chapter X <u>Mohawk Pottery Types</u> is possibly the
    most applicable portion of MacNeish's book. He mentions
    the works of Bailey at Chipman's Point, Vermont, and
    lists this site in his keyed map, pages 8 and 9.

                      Twenty-seven line drawings and thirty-
    three photographic plates make the text very clear.
    The bibliography takes up one page. There is an index.
    Naturally, in a work like this only pottery is dis-
    cussed.

                      (See also Bailey: "Iroquoian Ceramic
    Types," above.)

Title of Book: The Archaeology of Maine
Name of Author: Moorehead, Warren K.
Publisher: The Andover Press, Andover, Mass., 1922
Salient Features: Cloth bound, seven and a quarter inches
    wide, ten inches long, approximately three quarters of
    an inch thick; 272 pages; there is a four-page biblio-
    graphy and an index.

        Subtitle, A Report on the Archaeology of
of Maine (1912-1920) Together with Work at Lake
Champlain, 1917.

        "The Lake Champlain Survey of 1917" is
described on pages 241-250 and consists chiefly of remarks concerning the works of Professor George H.
Perkins, which see.

        The illustrations include one hundred and
twenty-three (123) figures, principally photographs of
sites, artifacts, etc. There are eleven (11) maps and
plans.

        This book is good browsing as well as
good archaeology.

Title of Book: The Bird-Stone Ceremonial
Name of Author: Moorehead, Warren K.
Publisher: Allen I. Vosburgh, Saranac Lake, N. Y.,
                    1899
Salient Features: This paper-covered book is nine inches
    wide by eleven inches long. Its thirty-one pages are
    profusely illustrated by means of drawings, "being an
    account of some singular prehistoric artifacts found
    in the United States and Canada." Some thirty-eight
    "birdstones" are shown.

Name of Book: <u>Prehistoric</u> Implements (A Reference Book)
Name of Author: Moorehead, Warren K., assisted by Professor
                   G. H. Perkins (UVM) and other experts.
Publisher: Robert Clarke Co., Cincinnati, Ohio
                   (Copyright 1900 by W. K. Moorehead)
Salient Features: "The professional archaeologists of museums
    will understand that this book is not for them."

        Dr. Moorehead apparently compiled this work
during his enforced stay at Saranac, New York, where for
more than three years he suffered from pulmonary tubercu-
losis.

        Professor George H. Perkins of UVM wrote
Section IV, Archaeology of New England, using many
illustrations from Vermont.

        Section X, St. Lawrence Basin and Canada
has considerable material applicable to Vermont.

        This book is cloth-bound, seven and a quarter
inches (7 1/4) wide, ten (10) inches long and almost one
(1) inch thick. There are six hundred and twenty-one
(621) illustrations and an index.

Title of Book: <u>Prehistoric Relics</u>
Name of Author: Moorehead, Warren K.
Publisher: The Andover Press, Andover, Mass., 1905
Salient Features: "Nearly all the collections of archaeo-
    logical specimens have at some time or other wished for
    an inexpensive, yet complete, illustrated catalog.

        "Recognizing the call for a collectors
book--one that should be for laymen and not for experts--
we have compiled this book, <u>Prehistoric Relics</u>. It is
solely for collectors and beginners; it is not intended
for museums or professionals."

        This is a paper covered book, six (6)
inches wide, nine and one half (9 1/2) inches long and
about one-half (1/2) inch thick. Its one hundred and
sixty-five (165) pages include one hundred and forty-
six (146) illustrations, carefully explained, and a
three (3) page bibliography. There is a good chapter
on collecting and arranging specimens.

Title of Article: "Archaeology of Ticonderoga"
Name of Author: Olsen, Godfrey J.
Name of Periodical: New York History, Vol. XV, No. 4,
                       October 1934, pages 407-411.
Salient Features: "What of the remoter past, before 1609
    (when Champlain visited Lake Champlain)?"

             "The Pells (owners of Fort Ticonderoga)
    have flatly refused to let us run a trench through their
    garden, or to tear down their residence, so that we
    might find out more about the Indian village which once
    occupied that area."

             "On the shore along the south side of
    the fort considerable evidence of aboriginal camps was
    found with artifacts both Algonkian and Iroquoian."

             Copper beads, stone arrow points, hard
    clam shells from the seashore, and other midden materials
    were found together with pottery sherds, hammers, etc.

             Several rock shelters were found on
    nearby Mount Defiance but these were not worked in 1934.

Title of Bulletins: Archaeological History of New York,
                     Parts 1 and 2
Name of Author: Parker, Arthur C.
Publisher: University of State of New York, New
                     York State Museum, Albany, N. Y.
                     July-August, September-October 1920.
                     (Bulletins 235, 236, 237, 238)
Salient Features: Part 1 contains material on the abori-
    ginal occupation of New York State; Evidences of
    Occupation; Various Sites. Part 2 gives Archaeological
    Localities in New York, by counties.

             Of chief interest to Vermont Investiga-
    tors are the sites along the New York-Vermont boundary
    from Pownal, Vermont, north to West Haven, Vermont, then
    along the shores of Lake Champlain. These are set forth
    in the several county maps of eastern upstate New York.

             Both parts of this work are carefully
    illustrated by means of maps, diagrams and photographs.
    Both parts have their own index; Part 2 has also six
    (6) pages of bibliography.

Birdstone Ceremonial Amulet (Actual size) from grave in
Addison County, Vermont. Authorities disagree on the
supposed uses of such a charm.

Celts from grave in Addison County, Vermont. (About one-
half actual size.)

Photographs courtesy of Museum of the American Indian, New York City

Title of Article: "The South Woodstock (Connecticut(Site"
Name of Author: Praus, Alexis A.
Name of Periodical: Bulletin of the Archaeological Society
                         of Connecticut, Number 17; March, 1945.
                         Pages 1-52.
Salient Features: This is par excellence a model of careful
     American Indian archaeology. Site descriptions, methods
     of excavation, analyses and classifications of findings
     are profusely illustrated with maps, drawings, diagrams,
     photographs and distribution charts. Not the least
     praiseworthy item is the large map folded into a pocket
     in the back cover of the book.

Title of Articles: "Aboriginal Remains in the Champlain
                        Valley"
Name of Author: Perkins, George H.
Name of Periodical: American Anthropologist
                        (1) Vol. XI, 1909, pp. 607-623;
                        (2) Vol. XIII, 1911, pp. 239-249;
                        (3) Vol. XIV, 1912, pp. 72-88.
Salient Features: In this extended paper Professor Perkins
    describes (1) Chipped objects, Gouges, Celts, Earthenware,
    Bone, Copper and Iron objects; (2) Grooved axes, prob-
    lematical objects such as pendants, stone amulets, bird
    stones, etc.; Flat, perforated stones or pierced tablets;
    Winged stones; Pick-shaped stones; Boat-shaped stones;
    Bar amulets; Discoidal stones, and Pipes; (3) Hammer
    stones and pestles; Clubs; Boiling stones; Mortars;
    Sinkers; Sinew stones; and Slate objects.

                    There are fifteen (15) full-page
    photographic illustrations of these aboriginal remains
    found in the Champlain Valley.

Title of Article: "Aboriginal Use of Bone in Vermont"
Name of Author: Perkins, George H.
Periodical: Science, October 7, 1892
Salient Features: "Bone objects are the rarest of archaeo-
    logical finds in the Champlain Valley. For many purposes,
    as awls and the like, bone would seem better suited than
    stone, and more easily worked." Probably bone was more
    commonly used than the collections seem to indicate.

Title of Article: "Archaeological Researches in the
                        Champlain Valley"
Name of Author: Perkins, George H.
Name of Periodical: Memoirs of the International Congress
                        of Anthropology. Chicago: Schulte
                        Publishing Company, 1894. Pages 84-94.
Salient Features: "The Champlain Valley, though of compara-
    tively inconsiderable area and containing neither mounds
    nor extensive village sites, has nevertheless yielded
    to diligent search many objects of considerable archaeo-
    logical interest.

                    "Archaeologically the Champlain Valley
    belongs with New York and the West rather than with
    New England the the East."

Title of Section: Archaeology of New England
Name of Author: Perkins, George H.
Name of Book: Prehistoric Implements, by W. K. Moorehead,
                   Robert Clarke Co., Cincinnati, Ohio,
                   Section IV.

                   Comments under <u>Prehistoric Implements</u>,
                   (a Reference Book) which see.

Title of Article: "Archaeology of Vermont"
Name of Author: Perkins, George H.
Periodical: The American Naturalist
                   Vol. XV, No. 6, June, 1881
Salient Features: Indian gouges "were not used for the pur-
    poses for which our modern gouges are designed" - at
    least, not all of them. Detailed descriptions of some
    ten gouges are given, together with drawings of same.
    "Bone gouges are common in the south; I have never seen
    any than a stone gouge in Vermont.

                "Some (gouges))may have been) used in
    excavating the charred portions of a log selected for a
    (dug out or) canoe, but it seems more probably that most
    (gouges) were used in one way or another in the process
    of preparing skins for clothing or for whatever other
    purposes the skins may have been needed."

Title of Article: "General Remarks upon the Archaeology of
                   Vermont"
Name of Author: Perkins, George H.
Periodical: Proceedings of the American Association
                   for the Advancement of Science, Vol.XXVLL,
                   St. Louis Meeting August 1878
Salient Features: "Rock inscriptions are rare....one at
    Bellows Falls, one at Brattleboro*... Pottery in frag-
    ments is common in the western part of the state; of
    entire jars (found) I know of only two. Pots of soap-
    stone occur rarely." Axes, chisels, pestles, scrapers,
    rimmers, knives, boatstones etc. occur. "Mounds like
    those in the west do not occur in Vermont."

 * See also Hall: Indians in Eastern Vermont

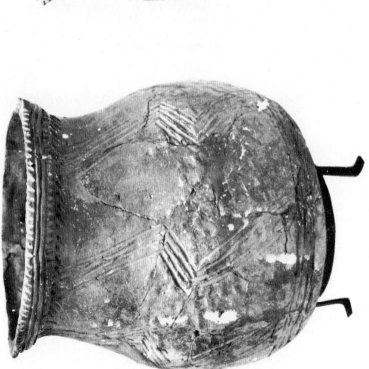

Iroquoian Pot, 7" high, from Addison County, Vt.   Algonkian Pot, 10¾" high, from Addison County, Vt.

Photographs courtesy of the Museum of the American Indian

New York City

Arrow points from Addison County, Vermont excavations.
Largest one, two and five eighths (2 5/8) inches long.
Photograph Courtesy of Museum of the American Indian, New York

Title of Article: "The Calumet in the Champlain Valley"
Name of Author: Perkins, George H.
Name of Periodical: Popular Science Monthly, pages 238-247.
                       Volume XIV, November to April, 1894.
                       D. Appleton Company, New York.
Salient Features: Professor Perkins describes in detail
   some stone pipes. "In beauty of material and in finish
   the pipes of the Champlain Valley are quite equal to the
   best of the mound pipes but in elaborateness of form they
   are much inferior.

               "Pipes, whether of stone or earthenware,
   are very uncommon in the Champlain Valley.

               "Most of the earthenware pipes of this
   region are very smooth on the outside."

               There are thirteen (13) drawings of various
   types of pipes found in the Champlain Valley.

Title of Article: "On Some Fragments of Pottery from Vermont"
Name of Author: Perkins, George H.
Periodical: Proceedings of the American Association for
                       the Advancement of Science, XXV, 1876,
                       pp. 325 - 335
Salient Features: "Most Vermont pottery is dark red or brown
   or black. Most of the jars found in Vermont are of compara-
   tively small size; one held twenty quarts, most are
   smaller." Most of the pottery described is from Essex,
   Chittenden county or not far from there.

        The ornamentation of all these jars is elaborate and
   artistic...So far as I can ascertain pots of steatite or
   any other stone are very rarely found in Vermont." But
   see letter from Dan Onion, Castleton, Vermont, June 9,
   1960, concerning Mr. Onion's discovery of a steatite pot
   near his home in Castleton, Spring 1951, when he was
   nine (9) years of age:
               "Since it was spring, the brook was high and
               the banks crumbling, but I did have to dig a
               little to find it. I remember that it was only
               a few feet below the surface of the bank. The
               only other material I found with it that might
               be Indian were small chunks of ochre. "The
               dish appears pock-marked. The inside walls are
               quite intact; the bottom has a <u>kill hole</u> in it.
               The stone is quite soft and can be scratched
               with the fingernail.

               "Its dimensions are, outside, 4" by 4 1/2"
               by 2 1/4" deep; inside, 2 1/4" by 2 1/2" by
               1 1/2" deep; the hole <u>kill</u>, oval shape, off
               center in bottom, 1 3/4" by 1".
   (Pots were ceremonially "killed" by punching holes in their
   bottoms, according to some legends.)

Title of Article: "On an Ancient Burial Ground in Swanton,
                      Vermont"
Name of Author: Perkins, George H.
Periodical: Proceedings of the American Association for
                     the Advancement of Science, Vol. XXII, 1873
                     pp. 76 - 100
Salient Features: "About two miles north of the village of
     Swanton, Vermont is a sandy ridge formerly covered by a
     dense growth of Norway pines. Rather more than twelve
     years ago (1861) it was discovered that beneath this
     forest stone implements were buried."

          The survivors of the St. Francis tribe, most recent
     aboriginal inhabitants, had no knowledge and no tradition
     of the ancient cemetery. "The sand in which the graves
     were dug is of a very light color, but that immediately
     around and beneath the body was, with two exceptions,
     colored a dark red or reddish brown; in the exceptional
     cases it was black. This red sand was from four to six
     inches in depth and its color was undoubtedly due to red
     iron oxide."

          "I am convinced that in the Swanton relics we have
     evidence that at some time a branch of the mound-building
     race wandered eastward."

          Copper implements, clay tubes, shell beads, stone
     tubes, perforated stones, carvings of animals and at
     least one discoidal stone were taken from the Swanton
     graves along with many arrow and spear points.

Title of Article: "Prehistoric Vermont--Evidences of Early
                      Occupation by Indian Tribes"
Name of Author: Perkins, George H.
Name of Periodical: Proceedings of the Vermont Historical
                      Society, 1905-1906, pages 89-101.
Salient Features: "Few evidences of long continued settle-
     ment have been found anywhere in the State (of Vermont).

          "No other New England State has given to
     the collector such variety of form and character, or
     such elegance of finish as may be found in any large
     collection of Vermont Indian relics."

          Professor Perkins describes several types
     of pottery and other artifacts in this article. There
     are no illustrations.

Title of Article: "Some Relics of the Indians of Vermont"
Name of Aughor: Perkins, George H.
Name of Periodical: American Naturalist, Volume V, 1871,
                        pages 11-17.
Salient Features: "The greater portion of the relics which
have been discovered were made from stone found in Vermont
but a few are of different material from anything found in
Vermont."

                   Relics described include arrow points,
pestles, mortars, axes, hatchets, pipes, pottery, pick
stones, and amulets. There are six (6) drawings of relics
mentioned.

Title of Article: "The Stone Ax in Vermont"; Celts or
                        Ungrooved
Name of Author: Perkins, George H.
Name of Periodical: The American Naturalist, Vol. XIX, Dec-
                        ember 1885, No. 12. Pages 1144-1149.
Salient Features: Celts or ungrooved axes are described in
This offering. "Celts are not uncommon in Vermont collections, and they exhibit a remarkable diversity in form,
size, material and workmanship....The average celt of the
Champlain Valley is about five inches long or a little
more, and half as wide.
                   "A second class of celts are quadrangular
in outline. A third class is narrower at one end than
the other, and the narrow edge, if there is but one edge,
is always that which is blunt."
                   There are seven (7) line drawings showing
the several kinds of celts mentioned.

Title of Article: "The Stone Ax in Vermont"; Notched and
                        Grooved Axes
Name Author: Perkins, George H.
Name of Periodical: The American Naturalist, Vol. XX,
                        April 1886. Pages 333-340.
Salient Features: "In all our collections we find a few
axes which are notched or grooved across the narrow sides.
They are not common in any portion of Vermont, nor, if
we may judge from what has been published by various
writers, do they appear to be abundant anywhere in the
United States.

                   "I do not think that archaeologists have
given the grooved ax sufficient credit, for utility as
a cutting instrument.

                   "In his account of a journey which he
took with a party of Algonkins in 1609, Champlain speaks
several times of the stone axes as used to fell trees,
and some of these were gros arbres."

                   This article is illustrated by means of
five (5) drawings of notched or grooved axes.

1, Boat Stone
2, 3, Bar Amulets
4, Copper bead necklace,
probably from Lake Superior region.
Unearthed in Addison County, Vt.
Photograph courtesy of Museum of the American Indian, New York

Title of Article: "Ground Slates: Eskimo or Indian?"
Name of Author: Ritchie, William A.
Periodical: Pennsylvania Archaeological Bulletin,
                   Vol. XXI, nos. 3-4, July - December 1959
Salient Features: "The cultural context responsible for the
    ground slate industry remained undiscovered until 1937
    when Bailey's excavations near Vergennes, Vermont and
    Ritchie's researches at Brewerton, New York brought to
    light much material so that Ritchie could formulate the
    Laurentian cultural aspect.

        "It thus appears that Dorset Eskimo could
    not have been the donor of the ground slate industry to
    the Laurentian."

Title of Article: "The Indian in His Environment"
Name of Author: Ritchie, William A.
Periodical: New York State Museum and Science Service,
                   Journal Series no. 10
Salient Features: But a single site attributed to each of
    three northeast states, Pennsylvania, Vermont and Massa-
    chusetts have had distinctive fluted points, etc.

        Nowhere in the eastern United States are
    Paleo Indian implements found with the bones of the
    animals they were used to kill.

Title of Book: Pre-Iroquoian Occupations of New York State.
Name of Author: Ritchie, William A.
Publisher: Rochester Museum of Arts and Sciences,
                Rochester, New York, 1944
Salient Features: This book is a MUST for persons seeking
    information concerning Pre-Iroquoian inhabitants not
    only of New York state, but probably of bordering states
    and Canada.

        Eight and one half inches (8 1/2) wide, eleven
    inches (11) long, one and one-half (1 1/2) inches thick,
    this book contains four hundred and sixteen (416) pages
    inclusive of a sixteen (16) page bibliography and an
    index of six (6) pages.

        Carefully illustrated by twenty (20) pages of
    tables, one hundred and sixty-five (165) plates and six
    (6) text-figures this monumental work covers everything
    from abrading stones and copper axes to Wabenaki, Willow
    Point and Zook.

        Bailey, Moorehead, Perkins, Skinner, Willoughby
    and others quoted in this Annotated Bibliography are
    mentioned by Ritchie in his book.

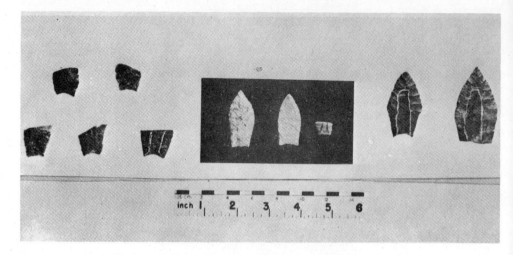

Fluted points from Reagen Component, Franklin, Vermont
(From Plate 15, Ritchie, Bulletin 358.)

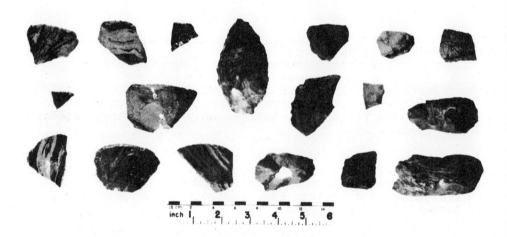

Retouched flake knives from Reagen Component, Franklin County,Vt.
(From Plate 14, Ritchie, Bulletin 358, New York State Museum,
Albany, New York, June 1957.)

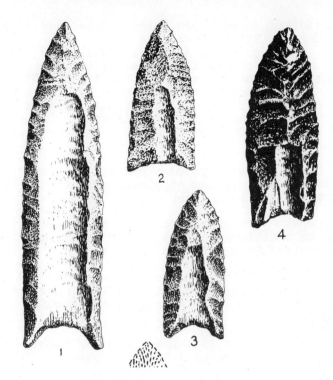

Fluted points from Rhode Island, 1, 2, 3; from Vermont, 4.

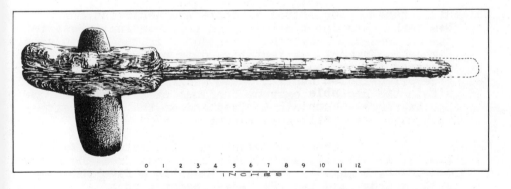

Ax or mace in original haft, found submerged off Penikese Island,
Massachusetts, August 1956.
Pictures on this page courtesy of Massachusetts Archaeological
Society.

Title of Article: "A Probable Paleo-Indian Site in Vermont"
Name of Author: Ritchie, William A.
Periodical: American Antiquity, Volume 18, No. 3,
                   January 1953, pages 249-258.
Salient Features: In this article Dr. Ritchie, State Archaeo-
     logist for New York, tells of the work of William A. Ross
     and Benjamin W. Fisher of St. Albans, Vermont, at the
     Reagen site, Highgate township, Franklin County, Vermont.
     State Geologist Charles G. Doll is given a special note
     of thanks.

          "The chipped stone industry of the Reagen
     site embodies a complex of piercing, cutting, scraping,
     and graving tools and weapons.

          "The Reagen component is unequivocally
     linked to that large constituent of early man sites
     characterized by a fluted point tradition.

          "In the temporal sequence of the Northeast,
     it (the Reagen site) may be found to occupy a position
     in the late paleo-Indian horizon, or sometime prior to
     4000 B.C."

          There is a plate showing eighty-seven (87)
     artifacts, and a two-page bibliography.

Title of Bulletin: Traces of Early Man in the Northeast
Name of Author: Ritchie, William A.
Publisher: New York State Museum and Science Service,
                   Albany, N. Y., June 1957. (Bulletin
                   Number 358.)
Salient Features: Dr. Ritchie, State Archaeologist for
     New York, sets forth material on paleo-Indian traces in
     the northeast. Prominently mentioned is the Reagen site,
     Highgate, Vermont. A tentative date of 5000 B. C. is
     assigned for the early existence of the "Champlain Sea";
     "the paleo-Indian hunters whose meager vestiges are found
     within the probable extreme confines of this sea--in the
     St. Lawrence--Champlain Lowland and at the Reagen site--
     must have been still more recent.

          There are eighteen (18) plates. Plates
     12, 13, 14, 15, 16, and 17 show artifacts from the Reagen
     Component, Highgate, Vermont. There is a five (5) page
     bibliography, and two (2) large inserted maps.

Title of Bulletin: "An Archaic Village in Middleboro,
                       Massachusetts" (Wapanucket No. 6)
Name of Author: Robbins, Maurice
Name of Publisher: Cohannet Chapter of Massachusetts
                       Archaeological Society, Inc., July 1959.

Salient Features: This bulletin includes everything from
the Last Will and Testament of Pamantaquash the Pond
Sachem, owner of the village site in 1668, to the last
detail of excavation.

            Humus, yellow soil, white sand, post
molds and lodge floors are noted. Pits, hearths, burials,
crematories, artifacts, and aberrant forms are described.
Adze blades, a grooved axe, plummets, atl-atl weights,
semi-lunar knives, bowl fragments, a wooden dish share
mention with metates, mullers, chipped axes and picks.

            Charts of vertical distribution are given.

            "From our work at Wapanucket Number Six
we have gained the impression of a people on the threshold
of significant advance. Their village was open and un-
defended. They did not fear molestation from others of
their kind."

            Three pages of bibliography, four maps
and eighteen plates testify to the painstaking thorough-
ness of this well designed archaeological investigation
of an Indian site of the 1600's and earlier.

Title of Guidebook: A Guidebook on Field Archaeology
Name of Author: Sargent, Howard R.
Publisher: New Hampshire Archaeological Society

Salient Features: "The writing of this guide was undertaken
    for the New Hampshire Archaeological Society in response
    to a long-felt need for a wider understanding of the
    methods of archaeology."

            "An attempt has been made to acquaint
    the reader with the fundamental principles of archaeology
    and to present the total framework within which the
    archaeologist must work."

            This guidebook presents Methods; Research
    Forms; Photo/Sketch Forms; Use of the Archaeological Site
    Survey Form; Site Code Numbers; Types of Archaeological
    Sites in New Hampshire (Villages; Camp sites; Rock
    Shelters; Quarries; Petroglyphs; Log dugouts; Cemeteries;
    Weirs; Buried sites; Colonial sites, etc.).

            With minor changes this Guidebook would
    serve very well for Vermont projects. Used together with
    Professor Burtt's "Proposed Classification for Identifi-
    cation Purposes" and Mr. Fowler's "Preliminary Classifi-
    cation Outlines," this guide would be a veritable
    "Archaeologist's Bible."

Title of Article: "Two Sites on the Baker River"
Name of Author: Sargent, Howard R.
Name of Periodical: The New Hampshire Archaeologist,
            Number six, 1956. Pages 6-9.

Salient Features: While the results are inconclusive, the
    first site investigated (July-August 1955) is probably
    not the ancient village of Asquamchumake; "the total ab-
    sence of pottery suggests that the site belongs to a
    pre-ceramic horizon."

            As for the second site, sherds and
    projectile points were found. However, more detailed
    examination of both sites would seem necessary.

            There is a map showing both Baker River
    sites, and a plate of line drawings illustrating the
    sherds taken from the Baker River situation.

Title of Article: "Review of Boylston Street Fishweir II"
Name of Author: Sargent, Howard R.
Name of Periodical: Bulletin of the Archaeological Society
                      of Connecticut, Number 2, June, 1950.
                      Pages 41-43.

Salient Features: This article is a review of Boylston
     Street Fishweir II, a study of the Geology, Paleobotany
     and Biology of a site on Stuart Street in the Back Bay
     District of Boston, Massachusetts. By Elso S. Barghoorn
     and others; edited by Frederick Johnston. Peabody Foun-
     dation for Archaeology, Vo. 4, No. 1. Phillips Academy,
     Andover, Mass., 1949.

               In 1939 and 1946 fishweir remains were
     found some twenty feet down in silt and peat in the Back
     Bay section of Boston.

               "The segments of the fishweir found thus
     far were constructed along the shore of an embayment
     around which people presumably lived. Estimates of the
     age of the weir vary between 2000 and 3600 years ago."

               "(This work) does, however, make a very
     significant contribution to our knowledge of climatic
     and environmental conditions....It also has succeeded
     in correcting the previously held idea that the climate
     was warmer at the time the fishweir was used."

Title of Article: "The Pickpocket Falls (New Hampshire) Site"
Name of Author: Sargent, Howard R.
Periodical: The New Hampshire Archaeologist, Number
                      Nine, September 1959. Pages 2-6.

Salient Features: "The Pickpocket Falls (N.H. 46-2) Site is
     located in the southwestern corner of Exeter, Rockingham
     County, New Hampshire.

               "A total of nine (9) features were examined,
     simple hearths, stone-lined hearths, refuse pit (?) a
     post mold, and intrusive post holes."

               Pottery and other artifacts were unearthed.
     The illustrations include a map of the site, a ground
     plan of the excavated area, pictures of potsherds and
     pictures of chipped stone artifacts.

               "The real significance of the Pickpocket
     Falls site has to do with the pottery it has produced
     and implications which it has for the culture-sequence
     in New Hampshire."

Title of Article: "Radiocarbon Dates and Their Bearing on
                      New Hampshire Archaeology"
Name of Author: Sargent, Howard R.
Name of Periodical: The New Hampshire Archaeologist, Number
                      Seven, March 1954. Pages 1-10.

Salient Features: Mention is made of clay varve counts,
     tree ring dating, etc., as not too satisfactory for esti-
     mating ages of sites, etc., in the New World.

                      Radiocarbon dating (in spite of limita-
     tions) now appears to be our most reliable tool for de-
     termining the age of archaeological deposits.

                      "With the high cost of processing a carbon
     sample one must be certain of the association as well as
     of the identification of the cultural horizon.....In a
     pre-ceramic site in North Hartland, Vermont, a large bed
     of charcoal and two dog skeletons have been excavated but
     proof is lacking of their direct association with the
     cultural debris."

                      The article is illustrated by means of
     two tables. There is a two-page bibliography.

                      (See also Briggs and Weaver: "How Old
     Is It?" elsewhere in this work.)

Title of Article: "Archaeological Specimens from New England"
Name of Author: Saville, Marshall H.
Periodical: Indian Notes and Monographs, Vol. V, No. 1,
                   Museum of the American Indian, New York,
                   1919.

Salient Features: In this ten (10) page booklet quotations
     are made from the (Boston) American Academy of Arts and
     Sciences, 1785, which tell of a stone ax, a gouge, a
     stone tobacco pipe and an emblematical stone, perhaps a
     carried pestle. Reference is made to the works of
     Professor George H. Perkins of U.V.M. especially his
     "Some Relics of the Indians of Vermont." There are
     two (2) illustrations depicting the objects mentioned
     here.

Title of Booklet: <u>Caves in Vermont</u> (A Spelunker's Guide to
                      Their Location and Lore)
Name of Author: Scott, John
Publisher: Kollooleet Independent Speleological Society,
                      Hancock, Vt.

Salient Features: This booklet gives locations of caves in
     Vermont, "the story of a group of summer campers, as well
     as a directory of Vermont caves."

           As yet no traces of aboriginal occupation
of caves proper have been found, although overhangs (rock
shelters) along Lake Champlain have yielded skeletal
remains and artifacts. (See Bailey: "A Rock Shelter at
Fort Ticonderoga" and "A Stratified Rock Shelter in
Vermont," above.)

           This booklet of 45 pages contains six (6)
maps, fifteen (15) photographs, one (1) page of bibliography and a four (4) page index.

Title of Article: "An Ancient Algonkian Fishing Village at
                   Cayuga, New York"
Name of Author: Skinner, Alanson B.
Periodical: Indian Notes and Monographs, Vol. II, No. 2,
                   Museum of American Indian, New York, 1919.

Salient Features: This work is described here because any
     possible Algonkian fishing sites in Vermont, when and if
     discovered and excavated, probably will show about the
     same characteristics as the one investigated at Cayuga.

           Skeletons, celts, arrowpoints, part of a
bear's jaw, decorated box-tortoise shells, stone sinkers,
a bone fish hook, bone harpoon points, hammerstones, net
sinkers, gouges, scrapers, arrowpoints, drills, Algonkian
potsherds and other Algonkian evidences are described
over fifteen (15) pages of text and illustrated by means
of ten (10) photographic plates.

Title of Article: "Identification of Important Sites in the
                    Northeast"
Name of Author: Smith, Benjamin L.
Periodical: Bulletin of the Massachusetts Archaeo-
                    logical Society, Inc., Vol. 21, No. 3 and 4,
                    April-July, 1960.

Salient Features: "Any site displaying one or more of the fol-
    lowing features should be reported, especially if it is
    threatened by destruction (as in road building or house
    construction) or looting.

1. Extensive areas of black greasy earth below the loam. (Indicates concentrated habitation area.)
2. Heavy concentrations of chips, artifacts, and other remains of obvious aboriginal character spread over an appreciable area.
3. Repeated occurrence of archaic types of blades: adz, gouge, ground slate ulu, plummet, etc.
4. Concentration of graves even if contents are not spectacular.
5. Ceremonial graves with unusual associated grave goods such as cache blades, powdered red ochre, potsherds and finely made articles.
6. Stone chips of unusual size, quantity or materials.
7. Fluted points.
8. Post molds.
9. Pottery.
10. Caches.

"Above all, try to keep information about the discovery out of local newspapers, for publicity is your worst enemy."

(In the same bulletin: Articles on New England sites; Recent world-wide sea level changes; Iroquoian-Mohawk pottery, etc.)

Title of Book: <u>Antiquities of the New England Indians</u>
Name of Author: Willoughby, Charles C.
Publisher: Peabody Museum of American Archaeology and
                   Ethnology, Harvard University, 1935

Salient Features: The best single volume work of its kind.
    This book stresses Pre-Algonkian, Old Algonkian and some
    of the beatures of the mixed Algonkian and Iroquoian
    cultures found in northwestern Vermont.

                The book is six and one quarter (6 1/4)
    inches wide, nine and one half (9 1/2) inches long and
    about one and one quarter (1 1/4) inches thick.   There
    are three hundred and fourteen pages, one hundred and
    forty six plates, and an excellent index.

                Mr. Willoughby drew considerably on the
    works of W.K. Moorehead, George H. Perkins and the
    collections at the University of Vermont. If this book
    could be brought up to date, using the findings of Ritchie
    and others, it would fill a great need.

Title of Article: "Distinguishing Characteristics of
                    Algonkian and Iroquoian Cultures"
Name of Author: Wintemberg, W. J.
Name of Periodical: National Museum of Canada Annual Report
                    for 1929; Bulletin No. 67.   Pages 65-125.
                    Ottawa, F. A. Acland, Printer to the
                    King's Most Excellent Majesty, 1931.

Salient Features: Although supplanted by more modern works,
    this presentation is one of the classics in comparative
    (or contrasting) treatment of distinguishing features in
    Algonkian and Iroquoian artifacts.

                Opening with an introduction by Diamond
    Jenness (whose book on the Indians of Canada has recently
    been reprinted) the article gives characteristics of
    Algonkian and Iroquoian sites, then discusses briefly
    stone work, copper artifacts, earthenware, bone, antler,
    teeth and shell artifacts and closes with a section on
    burials.

                There are fifteen (15) excellent photo-
    graphic plates and one (1) line-drawing.

                Vermont's northwestern counties were
    frequented by Iroquoians in historic times. Probably
    the works of Ritchie, Fowler and Sargent reviewed in
    this work, together with Willoughby's monumental book will
    help interested people to distinguish between Iroquoian
    and Algonkian artifacts in general: MacNeish's <u>Iroquois</u>
    <u>Pottery Types</u> is very useful for sherds, and even whole
    pots.